**Enforcement in the magistrates' courts:
a guide to enforcing money payments**

Fourmat Publishing

Enforcement in the magistrates' courts:
a guide to enforcing money payments

by
Ian S Lomax, LL.B, Barrister-at-Law
and
Steven Reynolds, LL.B, Barrister-at-Law

London
Fourmat Publishing
1988

ISBN 1 85190 045 4

First published in 1985 as *Arrears Proceedings*
by Barry Rose (Publishers) Ltd
This edition 1988

Part of the royalties on his book
have been donated to Vranch House, Exeter,
a school for handicapped children.

All rights reserved

© 1988 Fourmat Publishing
27 & 28 St Albans Place Islington Green London N1 0NX
Printed in Great Britain by
Billing & Sons Ltd, Worcester

Preface

Imprisonment for debt in England and Wales was abolished by Parliament in 1869. Despite this, our prisons currently contain approximately one thousand people who have been imprisoned for failure to pay a sum of money. The reason for this apparent contradiction is that whilst the Debtors Act 1869 abolished imprisonment for debt in general, it expressly retained it for a number of classes of default, namely fines, maintenance, rates, and certain instances of civil debt. In the context of the overall prison population, the number of debtors is small, but the issue is still of some social importance; these people may have reached prison not because they have committed offences for which the court would or could have imposed imprisonment as a fitting penalty, but because of their failure to comply with a monetary order of the court. Not surprisingly, the system has its critics and there are those who argue that in its effect upon a person's character, the suffering caused to family and dependants, the interruption of work, and the possibility of failing to find work upon release, the use of imprisonment is often out of all proportion to the wrong which has been committed, or the default. Others argue with equal vigour that imprisonment must be retained as the ultimate sanction and cannot be dispensed with if the integrity of the court and the credibility of its monetary orders are to be maintained.

It is not, however, the purpose of this book to debate the argument, but simply to explain the workings of the law as enacted by Parliament, and to ensure that when imprisonment is considered, it is done with full knowledge of all relevant statute and case law. Quite clearly, the courts are able, by the use of alternative powers, to deal effectively with the vast majority of defaulters who never go anywhere near a prison. It is these alternative powers with which this book is also concerned.

Since publication of the first edition we have been heartened by two events. The first is the large number of constructive comments made for the book's enhancement, many of which have been incorporated. The second is the wide acceptance afforded to the book by such diverse organisations as the courts, the police, the probation service, private practitioners and CABx.

We have taken the opportunity not only to bring many of the chapters up-to-date, but also, with the benefit of hindsight, to handle the subject matter in a different way. Thus, we have given particular attention to imprisonment, transfer of fine orders, High Court proceedings, the special provisions relating to servicemen, and fixed penalties.

The law is stated as at August 1988. The Criminal Justice Act 1988 makes a number of amendments to various statutory provisions. As far as possible these have been explained in the text at the relevant points, but it should be noted that they are not yet in force. Nevertheless these notes should serve as a useful guide highlighting the areas where change is imminent.

What is said in Chapter 11 about the enforcement of rates will remain valid in respect of rates, although new enforcement provisions will doubtless be introduced to deal with the community charge.

Ian S Lomax
Steven Reynolds
August 1988

Contents

		page
Chapter 1	**Fines, costs, compensation and forfeited recognizances**	1
	1. Introduction	1
	2. Requirement of notice	2
	3. Time for payment and payment by instalments	3
	4. Means inquiry	3
	5. Transfer of fine orders	4
	6. Money payments supervision order	8
	7. Distress warrants	10
	8. Crown Court fines	15
	9. Remission	15
	10. Power to search	18
	11. Juveniles	18
	12. Attendance centre orders	19
	13. Enforcement by High Court and county court	21
	14. Recording details of enforcement	22
	15. The Channel Islands and the Isle of Man	23
	16. Financial penalty enforcement orders—armed forces	23
	17. Fines imposed by coroners	24
	18. Fines on companies	24
	19. Civilian enforcement officers	24
Chapter 2	**Imprisonment and detention**	26
	1. Introduction	26
	2. Consecutive periods of imprisonment	27
	3. Postponement of issue of warrant	28
	4. Imprisonment at time of conviction	29
	5. Imprisonment on occasion after conviction	30
	6. Means inquiry	30
	7. Reduction of period of imprisonment	32
	8. Receipt of payments after imprisonment imposed	34
	9. Detention for short periods	34

	10. Execution in different parts of the United Kingdom of warrants for imprisonment for non-payment of fine	36
	11. Young persons	38
Chapter 3	**Confiscation orders**	39
	1. Drug trafficking	39
	2. Other powers to make confiscation orders	41
Chapter 4	**Fixed penalties**	44
	1. Introduction	44
	2. Registration of sums payable in default for enforcement as fines	44
	3. Challenging fine registration	47
Chapter 5	**General provisions relating to the enforcement of maintenance orders**	49
	1. Introduction	49
	2. Factors which may affect the enforcement of a maintenance order	51
	3. Procedures for enforcement	53
	4. The hearing	58
	5. Appeal	63
	6. Maintenance orders made against members of Her Majesty's Forces	64
	7. Visiting forces	66
Chapter 6	**Imprisonment for non-payment of maintenance**	68
	1. Introduction	68
	2. Restrictions on the use of imprisonment	68
	3. Restrictions on the detention of young persons	69
	4. The term of imprisonment	70
	5. Effect of committal on arrears	70
	6. Postponing a warrant of commitment	71
	7. Power to review committals	72
	8. Power to review where defendant already committed	73
	9. Payment after imprisonment imposed	76
Chapter 7	**Registration and enforcement of certain maintenance orders**	77
	1. Introduction	77
	2. Registration of a High Court or county court order in the magistrates' court	78
	3. Registration of magistrates' court order in the High Court	80
	4. Registration of English orders in Scotland and Northern Ireland	83

Contents

	5. Registration in England of maintenance orders made by courts in Scotland or Northern Ireland	87
Chapter 8	**Attachment of earnings**	91
	1. Introduction	91
	2. Application and procedure	92
	3. Power to obtain statement of earnings	93
	4. Power to make an order	94
	5. The order	95
	6. The employer	96
	7. The debtor	97
	8. Failure to comply with order	98
	9. Variation and discharge	98
	10. Lapse and discharge	102
	11. Power of court to determine whether payments are earnings	103
	12. Consolidated orders	104
	13. Cessation of order	105
	14. Priority between orders	106
	15. Service of orders and notices	107
Chapter 9	**Enforcement of legal aid contribution orders**	108
	1. Introduction	108
	2. Recovery by the collecting court	108
	3. Commencement of proceedings	109
	4. Procedure for recovery	109
	5. Transfer of enforcement proceedings to a different court	111
	6. Members of the armed forces	111
	7. Recovery in the High Court or county court	111
	8. Costs of a legally aided person paid by any other person	111
Chapter 10	**Civil debt**	113
	1. Introduction	113
	2. Sums recoverable as a civil debt	113
	3. Sums enforceable as a civil debt	115
	4. Distress	116
	5. Imprisonment	116
Chapter 11	**General rates**	120
	1. Introduction	120
	2. Distress	120
	3. Imprisonment owing to insufficient distress	124
	4. Water rates	128
Appendix 1:	Maximum terms of imprisonment: summary	131
Appendix 2:	Forms (listed at page 133)	132
Index		172

Table of abbreviations

AEA 1971	Attachment of Earnings Act 1971
CJA 1982	Criminal Justice Act 1982
CJA 1988	Criminal Justice Act 1988
GRA 1967	General Rate Act 1967
LAA 1974	Legal Aid Act 1974
LAA 1982	Legal Aid Act 1982
MCA 1980	Magistrates' Courts Act 1980
MC(AE)R 1971	Magistrates' Courts (Attachment of Earnings) Rules 1971
MC(E)R 1971	Magistrates' Courts (Earnings) Rules 1971
MC(F)R 1981	Magistrates' Courts (Forms) Rules 1981
MC(MOA 1958)R 1959	Magistrates' Courts (Maintenance Orders Act 1958) Rules 1959
MCR 1981	Magistrates' Courts Rules 1981
MOA 1950	Maintenance Orders Act 1950
MOA 1958	Maintenance Orders Act 1958
MOA 1950 (SJ)R 1950	Maintenance Orders Act 1950 (Summary Jurisdiction) Rules 1950
RAF(PCI)A 1951	Reserve and Auxiliary Forces (Protection of Civil Interests) Act 1951
RAF(PCI)R 1951	Reserve and Auxiliary Forces (Protection of Civil Interests) Rules 1951
TA 1982	Transport Act 1982
WA 1945	Water Act 1945
WA 1973	Water Act 1973

Table of cases

	page
Abley v Dale (1851) 15 JP 147	114
Allen v Allen [1985] Fam 8, [1985] 1 All ER 93, [1985] 2 WLR 65	63
Berry v Berry [1987] Fam 1, [1986] 2 All ER 948, [1986] 3 WLR 257 (CA)	63
Bidie, Re, Bidie v General Accident Fire and Life Assurance Corporation Ltd [1949] Ch 121, [1948] 2 All ER 995 (CA)	51
Board v Board (1981) 11 Fam Law 210, [1981] The Times 28 June	52
Bonaker v Evans [1850] 16 QB 162	14
Camden London Borough Council v Bromley Park Gardens Estates (1985) 84 LGR 367	122
Debtor, Re A (No 48 of 1952), ex parte Ampthill Rural District Council v The Debtor [1953] 1 All ER 545	114
Dickens v Pattison (1985) 15 Fam Law 163, (1985) 149 JP 271	61
Doncaster Metropolitan Borough Council v Lockwood [1987] The Times 15 January	122
Fildes (formerly Simkin) v Simkin [1959] 3 All ER 697	61
Fletcher v Fletcher [1985] 2 All ER 260, (1985) 15 Fam Law 192	63
Follick, Re, ex parte Trustee (1907) 97 LT 645	72
Forrest v Brighton Justices [1981] 2 All ER 711 (HL)	14, 28, 29, 31
Fowler v Fowler [1981] 2 FLR 141	71
Freeman-Thomas v Freeman-Thomas [1963] P 157, [1963] 1 All ER 17, [1963] 2 WLR 107	61
Goldschmidt v Oberrheinische Metallwerke [1906] 1 KB 373	22
Green (A Bankrupt), Re, ex parte Official Receiver v Cutting [1979] 1 All ER 832, [1979] 1 WLR 1211	51
Grocock v Grocock [1920] 1 KB 1	68
James v James [1964] P 303, [1963] 2 All ER 465, [1963] 3 WLR 331	51, 68
Johnson v Johnson [1946] 1 All ER 573	71
Kendal v Wilkinson (1855) 19 JP 467	52
Kinning, ex parte [1847] 10 QB 730	114
Locker v Stockport Metropolitan Borough Council (1984) 15 Fam Law 189	122
Luscombe v Luscombe [1962] 1 All ER 668, [1962] 1 WLR 313 (CA)	51
Miles v Miles [1979] 1 All ER 865, [1979] 1 WLR 371	92
Mills v Mills (1982) 12 Fam Law 174	63
O'Connor v Isaacs [1956] 2 QB 288, [1956] 2 All ER 417, [1956] 3 WLR 172	54

xi

Parry v Meugens (1985) 150 JP 152, (1986) 16 Fam Law 53, [1986] 1 FLR
125 62
Pilcher v Pilcher (No 2) [1956] 1 All ER 463, [1956] 1 WLR 298 61
R v Avon Magistrates' Courts Committee, ex parte Bath Law Society
[1987] The Times 28 July 6
R v Bexley Justices, ex parte Floyd Henry [1971] RR 145 126
R v Birmingham Justices, ex parte Bennett [1983] 1 WLR 114, (1983) 147
JP 279 .... 10, 26, 31, 118
R v Birmingham Justices, ex parte Mansell [1988] The Times 7 May 126
R v Blackpool Justices, ex parte Ardullis [1981] The Times 21
December 62
R v Clacton Justices and Another, ex parte Commissioners of Customs
and Excise [1987] The Times 5 October 31
R v Clerkenwell Stipendiary Magistrates, ex parte Mays [1975] 1 All ER
65, [1975] 1 WLR 52 10
R v Colchester Justices ex parte Wilson [1985] AC 750, [1985] 2 All ER
97, (1985) 81 Cr App R 158 (HL) 5, 28, 29, 118, 127, 128
R v Dover Magistrates' Court, ex parte Kidner [1983] 1 All ER 475,
(1983) 13 Fam Law 208 .... 60, 62, 63
R v Durham Justices (1891) 55 JP 277 52
R v Ealing Justices, ex parte Coatsworth (1980) 124 SJ 274, (1980) 78
LGR 439 125
R v Edgehill [1963] 1 All ER 181 .... 84, 102
R v German (1891) 5 JP 358 10
R v Governor of Bedford Prison, ex parte Ames [1953] 1 All ER 1002,
[1953] 1 WLR 607 71
R v Halifax Justices, ex parte Woolverton (1978) 123 SJ 80, (1979) LS Gaz
129 61
R v Horseferry Road Magistrates' Court, ex parte Bernstein (1987) 151 JP
56, (1986) 150 JPN 799 63
R v Manchester City Magistrates' Court, ex parte Davies [1988] 1 All ER
930 126
R v Midhurst Justices, ex parte Seymour [1983] 5 Cr App R (S) 99, (1983)
147 JP 266 (CA) 27
R v Miskin Lower Justices, ex parte Young [1953] 1 QB 533, [1953] 1 All
ER 495, [1953] 2 WLR 409 71
R v Norwich Justices, ex parte Tigger (formerly Lilly) [1987] The Times
26 June 31, 118
R v Poole Justices, ex parte Fleet [1983] 2 All ER 929, [1983] 1 WLR
974 .... 127, 128
R v Southampton Justices, ex parte Davies [1981] 1 All ER 722, [1981] 1
WLR 374 27
R v Wilmot (1861) 25 JP 596 52
Ratford and Hayward v Northavon District Council [1986] 3 All ER 193,
[1986] 3 WLR 771 122
Ross v Pearson [1976] 1 All ER 790, [1976] 1 WLR 224 61
Russell v Russell (1985) 16 Fam Law 156, [1986] 1 FLR 465 (CA) 61

Table of cases

Sammy-Joe v GPO Mount Pleasant Office and Another [1966] 3 All ER 924, [1967] 1 WLR 370 52
Shillitoe v Hinchcliffe (1922) 86 JP 110 121
Slater v Calder Justices [1984] 5 FLR 719, (1984) 148 JP 129 ...... 73, 74, 75
Smith v Smith (1976) 6 Fam Law 245 79
Snape v Snape (1983) 13 Fam Law 210 63
Starkey v Starkey [1954] P 449, [1954] 1 All ER 1036, [1954] 2 WLR 907 71
Streames v Copping [1985] QB 920, [1985] 2 All ER 122, [1985] 2 WLR 993 63
Thaha v Thaha (1987) 17 Fam Law 234, [1987] 2 FLR 142 82
Verall v Hackney London Borough Council [1983] QB 445, [1983] 1 All ER 277, [1983] 2 WLR 202 (CA) 121
Wood v Warley Justices (1974) 4 Fam Law 130 73
Wood v Wood [1957] P 254, [1957] 2 All ER 14, [1957] 2 WLR 826 (CA) 51

Chapter 1

Fines, costs, compensation and forfeited recognizances

1. Introduction

This chapter concerns securing payment of sums required to be paid upon conviction or by order of the court, described as "Sums adjudged to be paid by a conviction". These comprise:

(a) fines;
(b) orders for costs;
(c) compensation orders; and
(d) forfeited recognizances.

Generally, the procedure is the same in all four cases; differences are pointed out in the text.

Before going on to consider in detail the various methods of recovery, it is appropriate to say that without doubt the first step towards effective enforcement must be the setting by the bench of the fine at a realistic level appropriate to the means of the offender. It is now firmly established that, save in exceptional circumstances, fines, costs and compensation should be capable of being paid within a period of twelve months. It is a wholly self-defeating exercise to set a fine which is too high, and then to go on to order payments which an offender patently cannot afford or which result in an over-long period during which those payments are to be made. Default is almost bound to occur creating virtually insoluble problems for the court later.

Where default is made in payment of a fine, costs, compensation or forfeited recognizance, the options available to the court are:

(a) allowing time to pay or payments by instalments (see page 3);
(b) variation of instalments (see page 3);
(c) a transfer of fine order (see page 4);

(d) a money payments supervision order (see page 8);
(e) issue of a distress warrant (see page 10);
(f) remission (see page 15);
(g) search for money (see page 18);
(h) where the defaulter is a juvenile, steps against his parents may be taken (see page 18);
(i) an attendance centre order (see page 19);
(j) enforcement in the High Court or county court (see page 21);
(k) committal to prison (see Chapter 2);
(l) an attachment of earnings order (see Chapter 7).

Options (a) to (j) are considered below.

It must always be remembered, however, that in relation to compensation, enforcement proceedings are precluded until a period of twenty-one days has elapsed from the date of the making of the order (s 36(2)(a) Powers of Criminal Courts Act 1973). In other cases, proceedings can be taken immediately.

2. Requirement of notice

When a sum is adjudged to be paid by summary conviction and:

(a) the court has allowed time for payment; or
(b) the court has directed payment by instalments; or
(c) the offender is absent, when the sum to be enforced is imposed,

the clerk of the court must serve on the offender notice in writing stating the amount of the sum imposed and, if it is to be paid by instalments, the amount of the instalments, the date on which the sum or each of the instalments is to be paid, and the place and times at which payment may be made (r 46 Magistrates' Courts Rules 1981 ("MCR 1981")).

This requirement also applies where a magistrates' court is required to enforce a fine imposed or recognizance forfeited by the Crown Court (see page 15).

The notice is to be served by delivering it to the offender or by sending it to him by post in a letter addressed to him at his last known or usual place of abode.

Form 46 in the Magistrates' Courts Forms Rules 1981 is the prescribed form of notice.

If the procedure described above has not been followed, enforcement proceedings cannot be brought.

3. Time for payment and payment by instalments

The court before which a sum is adjudged to be paid by a conviction may require immediate payment, allow time for payment, or order payment by instalments.

Where time for payment has been allowed, as distinguished from payment by instalments, the court or justices' clerk may, on application by or on behalf of the person liable to make the payments, allow further time to pay or order payment by instalments (s 75(2) MCA 1980).

Application for time for payment may be made in writing. The applicant need not attend the hearing unless the court so requires (r 51 MCR 1981).

The application does not have to be made by the person liable to make payment, but may instead be made on his behalf. This enables applications to be made by persons such as parents, husbands and wives, and probation officers.

Where payment by instalments has been ordered and default is made in payment of any one instalment the total amount outstanding may be enforced (s 75(3) MCA 1980).

Where the court originally ordered payment by instalments, it may, on application of the person liable to pay the outstanding sum, vary the number of instalments payable, the amount of any instalment payable, and the date on which any instalment becomes payable (s 85A MCA 1980).

In this case the application must be made by the person liable to make payment and not by a person on his behalf.

4. Means inquiry

It is also open to the court, when allowing time to pay or ordering payment by instalments, to fix a date when the offender must attend court if, at that time, any instalment falling due remains unpaid; or, where time for payment has been allowed, any part of the original sum remains unpaid (s 86(1) MCA 1980). The purpose of the defendant's attendance at court will be for an enquiry to be made into his means, and for the court to consider why default has been made in payment. At such a hearing, the court may allow further time to pay or vary the rate of payments.

ENFORCEMENT IN THE MAGISTRATES' COURTS

As will be seen later (see page 30), although imprisonment may ultimately be imposed for failure to pay, the power to impose imprisonment may only be exercised after an inquiry into the defendant's means, subject to limited exceptions. Attendances at court at a hearing fixed in advance as above will qualify as a means inquiry for this purpose.

The power to fix in advance a date upon which the defendant is to return to court is one which may be exercised at the time of conviction, or at a later date, but only in the presence of the defendant. However, the court may, in the absence of the offender, fix a later day in substitution for the day originally fixed (s 86(2) and (3) MCA 1980). This power may be exercised by a single justice or by the justices' clerk (Justices' Clerks Rules 1970). Notice in writing of the substituted day must be served on the offender. Service may be effected in the same way in which service of a summons may be effected (r 52 MCR 1981).

Should an offender fail to appear in person on the day fixed under either of the above provisions and any part of the sum remains unpaid or an instalment which has fallen due remains unpaid, the court may issue a warrant to bring him before the court (s 86(4) MCA 1980).

Where, however, a later day has been fixed in the absence of the offender, in substitution for a day previously fixed, a warrant must not be issued unless it is proved to the court, on oath, or in such manner as may be prescribed, that notice in writing of the substituted day was served on the offender not less than what appears to the court to be a reasonable time before that day (s 86(5) MCA 1980).

5. Transfer of fine orders

Although known as "transfer of fine" orders, the orders discussed here may be made in respect of all four types of sum — fines, costs, compensation and forfeited recognizances.

(a) England and Wales

Where it appears to the convicting court that a defendant resides within the area of another court, the convicting court (or justices' clerk) may make a transfer of fine order making payment enforceable by the other court. The effect is to transfer from one court to another all functions relating to the collection and enforcement of any sum adjudged to be paid by a conviction. However, in the case of persons under the age of seventeen, the

Fines, costs, compensation and forfeited recognizances

power to make an order requiring a parent or guardian to enter a recognizance to ensure that a sum outstanding is paid, or an order directing a parent or guardian to pay an outstanding sum (see page 18), may not be transferred (s 89(1), (2) and (4) MCA 1980).

Once made there is no mechanism by which a transfer of fine order can be revoked or "withdrawn" even though it may later turn out that the defendant has never lived in the area of the other court. All that is required to give jurisdiction for the making of an order is that it should appear to the transferring court that the person "resides" in the area of the court. The court of transfer may not simply return the order to the original court because in its view the defendant does not live within the area. But if it appears to the court of transfer that the offender is residing within the area of another court again, a further transfer of fine order can be made (s 89(3) MCA 1980).

The words of s 89 MCA 1980, which empower courts to make transfer of fine orders, are clear and unambiguous and are not subject to any limitation or restriction upon transfer "only in certain circumstances". Thus, it is submitted, a transfer of fine order can be made even where a defendant has been committed to prison in default of payment and the issue of the warrant of commitment postponed (see page 28); the court of transfer in the event of default then has power to issue the warrant of commitment, this being a function transferred under the order. The statute itself overrides any difficulty where one court imposes imprisonment and another issues the warrant. It is also submitted that, in the light of the decision of the House of Lords in *R v Colchester Justices, Ex Parte Wilson* (1985), it is not only possible but essential that courts are able to transfer fines and other sums adjudged where imprisonment has been imposed in default. It may be that a defendant is living some distance from the original court once the warrant of commitment falls to be issued. In such a case it is in his interests and consistent with the spirit of the judgment of the court in the *Colchester Justices* case that he should be able to appear before a court to show cause why the warrant should not be issued. He will be much better able to do this if the court is local. It may be that there is considerable force in the argument that where a defendant subject to a postponed commitment has moved to another area and the warrant falls to be issued, then not only can the fine be transferred but it should be. For a fuller discussion on warrants of commitment and their postponement, see Chapter 2.

Furthermore, s 72A of the Magistrates' Courts Act 1952, now repealed and replaced by s 90 of the Act of 1980, formerly provided that a transfer of fine order to Scotland could be made except where a term of imprisonment had been fixed — a clear restriction on the power to transfer was there set out for all to see. By contrast, s 72 of that Act, concerning transfers within England and Wales, contained no such restriction. If it is to be said that nevertheless the effect in each case was the same, then the words of prohibition in the one case were at the very least superfluous. It is submitted that this was not the intention of Parliament and that the words were not superfluous. A difference between the two situations was clearly intended to exist and did so exist. In the one case a transfer of fine order could be made after imprisonment had been fixed but in the other it could not.

Although the Act of 1952 has been repealed, s 89 of the 1980 Act replaces the former provision and save for one exception is identical. The effect, it is submitted, is as before; and it is interesting to note that s 90 MCA 1980, which deals with transfers to Scotland and Northern Ireland, no longer contains any words of prohibition. The absence of words of prohibition recently fell to be considered by the High Court in the case of *R v Avon Magistrates' Courts Committee Ex parte Bath Law Society* (1987). It was held that, although there had been some doubt in the past, as there was nothing in the MCA 1980 to prevent a justice remanding a defendant to any court within a county, the practice was therefore lawful. While this is not direct authority in relation to transfer of fines it is a case where in the absence of words of prohibition the High Court has ruled that an action could be taken. By analogy the same principle could be applied to a transfer of fine order.

These provisions relate only to the transfer of a sum adjudged to be paid by a conviction. They do not refer to a legal aid contribution order for which separate provision is made (see page 111).

(b) Scotland and Northern Ireland

Where it appears to a magistrates' court that a person liable to pay a sum adjudged to be paid by a conviction is residing within the area of a court of summary jurisdiction in Scotland or within any petty sessions district in Northern Ireland the court may order that payment of the sum shall be enforced by the court responsible for the area in which the offender resides (s 90 MCA 1980).

A court may now make such an order even when a term of imprisonment in default of payment has been imposed.

The order must specify the court of summary jurisdiction by which or petty sessions district in which the payment of the sum is to be enforced. Where payment is to be enforced in Scotland and the sum involved is more that £100 or is a fine imposed by the Crown

Court or the Sheriff Court, the court to be specified must be the Sheriff Court and not a district court (s 90(2) MCA 1980).

From the date of the making of the order all functions that relate to satisfaction and enforcement which would have been exercisable by the court making the order will cease (s 90(3) MCA 1980). The power to make orders against parents or guardians in the case of persons under seventeen years of age may not be exercised by the court of transfer.

In the case of a transfer from Scotland or Northern Ireland under which payment is to be enforced in a magistrates' court in England and Wales, the court specified in the order as the responsible court will have all functions as if the sum transferred had been imposed by that court and as if any order made in relation to the sum before the transfer of fine order had been made also by that court (s 91(1) MCA 1980). Again, however, there will be no power to make orders against parents and guardians in respect of persons under seventeen years of age.

In relation to a sum originally imposed by the Crown Court transferred to Scotland or Northern Ireland and back again, the magistrates' court receiving the order has all the powers of enforcement as if the fine had been sent by the Crown Court under s 32(1) Powers of Criminal Courts Act 1973 (see page 15). In addition, any order made before the transfer in respect of the sum transferred by the court in Scotland or Northern Ireland is to be treated as if made by the court having power to enforce the outstanding sum (s 91(3) MCA 1980). There is no power to make orders against parents or guardians in the case of juveniles.

Form 60 in the Magistrates' Courts Forms Rules is the prescribed form of transfer of fine order to Scotland or Northern Ireland.

(c) Procedure

The clerk of the court making a transfer of fine order, or further transfer of fine order, is required to send to the court of transfer:

- (i) a copy of the order;
- (ii) a statement of the offence and the steps, if any, taken to recover the sum adjudged to be paid;
- (iii) such further information as is available and is likely to assist the court to which payment is transferred.

    (r 57 MCR 1981).

A copy of the order is also required to be sent to the clerk of the court in Scotland or Northern Ireland which originally imposed the fine.

The clerk of a magistrates' court receiving a transfer of fine order whether made in England and Wales, Scotland or Northern Ireland, is required, thereupon, if possible, to deliver or send by post to the offender notice in the prescribed form. Form 61 in the Magistrates' Courts Forms Rules 1981 is the prescribed form of notice.

Any moneys collected under a transfer of fine order are dealt with as if the collecting court had made the original order. But, where a fine is transferrred to a court in England and Wales from a court in Scotland or Northern Ireland, then:

(i) if the sum is paid, the clerk of the court of transfer is required to send the payment to the clerk of the court in Scotland or Northern Ireland; or

(ii) if the sum is not paid, the clerk is required to inform the clerk of the court in Scotland or Northern Ireland of the manner in which the adjudication has been satisfied, or that the sum or any balance thereof appears to be irrecoverable.

(r 57(4) MCR 1981).

Similarly, moneys collected in Scotland or Northern Ireland by the enforcing court should be returned to the court in England which made the transfer of fine order and therefore the sum should not be written off at the time of transfer.

6. Money payments supervision order

(a) The order

Where a person is adjudged to pay a sum by summary conviction, the court may, either at the time of conviction or subsequently, order him to be placed under the supervision of such person as the court appoints (s 88 MCA 1980). This is entirely at the discretion of the court and will be most appropriate in cases involving juveniles and young persons, or where it appears that the support and encouragement of someone else at hand may be productive in ensuring payment. Such an order may well avoid the need to consider more severe remedies.

The order places upon the person appointed supervisor the duty to advise and befriend the offender with a view to inducing him to pay the sum adjudged to be paid and thereby avoid committal to

Fines, costs, compensation and forfeited recognizances

prison for non-payment (see Chapter 2). The supervisor is under a duty to provide to the court any information that may be required relating to the offender's conduct and means (r 56 MCR 1981).

The person appointed supervisor will generally be a probation officer, but this need not always be the case. The court has a discretion, and may even appoint a close friend or relative, but it should be satisfied as to the suitability of the person it wishes to appoint. However, there is no power to require the appearance in court of the proposed supervisor.

The consent of the offender to the making of an order is not required and where an order is made on an occasion subsequent to the date of conviction, the presence of the offender is not necessary.

Should the court make an order in the absence of the offender, the clerk must deliver or send to him written notice in the prescribed form. Notice to the person appointed supervisor in these circumstances would be appropriate.

Form 62 in the Magistrates' Courts Forms Rules 1981 is the prescribed form of notice.

(b) Cessation of order

An order will continue in force as long as the offender remains liable to pay any outstanding balance. An order will cease on the making of a transfer of fine order. An order may be discharged by the court which made the order, but this does not preclude the court from making a subsequent order.

(c) Supervision and imprisonment

Where an order is in force, the supervised person must not be committed to prison in default of payment or for want of sufficient distress to satisfy the sum adjudged to be paid (see page 30), unless the court has taken such steps as may be reasonably practicable to obtain from the supervisor an oral or written report of the offender's conduct and means (s 88(6) MCA 1980). The report would provide the court with details of the defendant's behaviour, and of his income and expenditure throughout the period of supervision.

The fact that a person has been committed to prison in default of payment and the issue of the warrant of commitment postponed (see page 28), does not prevent the court making a money payments supervision order. However, in these circumstances the making of a money payments supervision order does not mean

9

that a report *must* be obtained from the supervisor before the warrant of commitment can be issued in the event of default, although it would be wise to do so. The requirement to obtain a report from the supervisor applies only at the stage when the term of imprisonment is originally fixed; it does not apply to the act of issuing the warrant in default of the terms of postponement (*R* v *Clerkenwell Stipendiary Magistrate, ex parte Mays* (1975)).

(d) Young persons

A court may not commit a person under twenty-one years of age for default of payment, on an occasion subsequent to conviction, unless that person has been placed under supervision, or the court is satisfied that it is undesirable or impracticable to place him under supervision (s 88(4) MCA 1980).

Where the court does commit a person under twenty-one years of age in default of payment without having placed him under supervision the court must state the grounds upon which it is satisfied that supervision is undesirable or impracticable in the warrant of commitment (s 88(5) MCA 1980).

7. Distress warrants

(a) Introduction

In recent years the use of distress warrants has undergone something of a resurgence. This is probably because of a number of factors. The first is a reluctance by the police to become involved in the enforcement of debt of whatever description. The second reason is the creation of the extended fixed penalty system, which provides the magistrates' court with a large number of low value debts to enforce. Third, the firms of private bailiffs themselves have not been slow to realise the commercial potential for growth and have marketed their services with increasing effectiveness. Finally, it should not be forgotten that the appeal courts have also encouraged the greater use of distress when emphasising that custody is a last resort only after all other methods have failed (see, for example, *R* v *Birmingham Justices ex parte Bennett* (1983)). However, justices may properly require positive evidence that the defendant has goods before issuing a warrant of distress (*R* v *German* (1891)).

The concept of distress is not new and it simply means the seizing of money and/or goods belonging to the debtor to satisfy his debt(s). The critics of the procedure claim it is an anachronism more in keeping with the financial times of Dickens than of the

Fines, costs, compensation and forfeited recognizances

1980s. The courts, however, whilst accepting it is not the answer to all their problems, see it as a useful part of their enforcement armoury. Unlike the county courts, the magistrates' courts do not certify bailiffs, so a firm of private bailiffs must be employed. While the police *can* execute distress warrants, it is unlikely that they will do so save in exceptional circumstances. One major benefit to the court of using private bailiffs is that they do not usually charge their costs to the court but simply add them to the debt requiring to be collected. Unfortunately, not all distress warrants are successful and many are returned "nulla bona", "no trace" or "sufficient goods but entry not achieved". There is currently a debate about the payment of bailiffs' costs by the court in such cases, for there is no provision to meet these costs out of public funds. See page 136 for the form of return.

(b) Issue and execution

The issue and execution of distress warrants is regulated by the MCA 1980 and MCR 1981, in particular, s 76 MCA 1980. As in the case of imprisonment, the court has power to postpone the issue of the distress warrant until such time and on such conditions, if any, as the court thinks fit (s 77(1) MCA 1980). Rule 54 MCR 1981 adds the necessary detail as to what the warrant must contain and how it is to be executed, namely:

(1a) The warrant must name or otherwise describe the person against whom the distress is to be levied.

(1b) The warrant must be directed to the constables of the police area in which the warrant is issued or to the authorised persons for the police area specified in the warrant, or to a person named in the warrant, and shall require them to levy the sum in question by distress and sale of the goods belonging to the person in question.

(1c) The warrant may, where it is directed to the constables of a police area, instead of being executed by any of those constables, be executed by any person under the direction of a constable.

(2) The warrant must authorise the person charged with the execution of it to take, as well as goods, any money of the person against whom the distress is levied; and any money so taken shall be treated as if it were the proceeds of the sale of goods taken under the warrant.

(3) The warrant must require the person charged with the execution to pay the sum levied to the clerk of the court that issued the warrant. Any wilful retention of the

proceeds (regardless of whatever offences were committed) is punishable by a fine (s 78(5) MCA 1980).

(4) There cannot be taken under the warrant the clothes or bedding of any person or his family or the tools and implements of his trade. However, if the tools and implements exceed £150 in value, it is lawful to take such of the tools etc as will leave in that person's possession tools and implements of his trade to the prescribed value. Note that water, gas and electricity fittings let for hire by the utility boards cannot be the subject of distress, and nor can Crown property.

(5) The distress levied under the warrant must be sold within such period beginning not earlier than the sixth day after the making of the distress as may be specified in the warrant; or, if no period is specified in the warrant, within a period beginning on the sixth day and ending on the fourteenth day after the making of the distress. However, with the consent in writing of the person against whom the distress is levied the distress may be sold before the beginning of the said period.

(6) The distress must be sold by public auction or in such other manner as the person against whom the distress is levied may in writing allow.

(7) The distress must not be sold if the sum for which the warrant was issued and the charges of taking and keeping the distress have been paid.

(8) Subject to any direction to the contrary in the warrant, where the distress is levied on household goods, they cannot, without the consent in writing of the person against whom the distress is levied, be removed from the house until the day of sale. However, the goods are impounded by affixing to the articles concerned a conspicuous mark. Removing the goods marked in this way, or defacing or removing the mark, is an offence (s 78(4) MCA 1980).

(9) The constable or bailiff charged with the execution of the warrant must cause the distress to be sold, and may deduct out of the amount realised by the sale all costs and charges incurred in effecting the sale. He must then return to the owner any balance, after retaining the amount for which the warrant was issued, and the proper costs and charges of the execution of the warrant.

Fines, costs, compensation and forfeited recognizances

(10) The constable or bailiff charged with the execution of the warrant must, as soon as is practicable, send to the clerk of the court that issued it a written account of the costs and charges incurred in executing it. The clerk must allow the person against whom the distress was levied to inspect the account within one month after the levy of the distress at any reasonable time to be appointed by the court. Note also that it is an offence to exact excessive charges and costs (s 78(5) MCA 1980).

(11) If any person pays or tenders to the constable or bailiff the sum mentioned in the warrant, or produces a receipt of that sum given by the clerk of the court that issued the warrant, and also pays the amount of the costs and charges of the distress up to the time of the payment or tender or the production of the receipt, the constable or bailiff must not execute the warrant, or must cease to execute it, as the case may be.

Despite the above requirements, if the warrant does contain any defect, this will not make it void, provided the warrant states that the sum has been adjudged to be paid by the conviction or order of a magistrates' court (s 78(1) MCA 1980). Similarly, a person acting under a warrant of distress is not deemed to be a trespasser by reason only of any irregularity in the execution of the warrant.

In addition to the statutory requirements detailed above, many courts also have local policies, such as the taking of part-payment by bailiffs, and imposing a time limit on the life of the warrant. These vary from area to area.

(c) Special provisions relating to the recovery of fines imposed on master, crew etc of a fishing boat

Where a fine is imposed by a magistrates' court in England and Wales or Northern Ireland on the master, owner, charterer or a member of the crew of a fishing boat who is convicted of an offence under s 5 or s 10 Sea Fisheries Act 1968 or s 2 Fishery Limits Act 1976, the court may:

(i) issue a warrant of distress against the boat, its gear, catch and any property of the person convicted, for the purpose of levying the amount of the fine; and

(ii) if the boat is a "foreign fishing boat", order it to be detained for a period not exceeding three months from the date of the conviction, or until the fine is paid, or the amount levied in pursuance of any distress warrant, whichever first occurs.

Section 77(1) MCA 1980 (postponement of issue) and s 78 MCA 1980 (defects in warrant of distress) apply. See s 12 Sea Fisheries Act 1968.

(d) Scotland and the Isle of Man

A warrant of distress issued in England can be executed in Scotland if endorsed in accordance with the Summary Jurisdiction (Process) Act 1881. This also applies to the Isle of Man by virtue of the Summary Jurisdiction Process (Isle of Man) Order 1928.

(e) Requirement to give notice, means inquiry etc

The issue of a distress warrant is not subject to the restrictions that apply in the case of imprisonment (see pages 29–30). Inquiry into means is not required before the issue of a warrant of distress. It seems that all that is necessary before the warrant is issued is a failure to comply with the terms of the order for payment.

In the absence of a specific provision giving the offender the right to be heard before a warrant is issued, as is the case before imprisonment, it might be argued that there is no such right. On the other hand, natural justice seems to imply such a right. Lord Fraser, giving the leading judgment of the House of Lords in the case of *Forrest* v *Brighton Justices* (1981), said:

> "One of the principles of natural justice is that a person is entitled to adequate notice and opportunity to be heard before any judicial order is pronounced against him, so that he, or someone acting on his behalf, may make such representations, if any, as he sees fit. This is the rule of *audi alteram partem* which applies to all judicial proceedings, unless its application to a particular class of proceedings has been excluded by Parliament expressly or by necessary implication."

In *Bonaker* v *Evans* (1850) it was said that:

> ". . . no proposition can be more clearly established than that a man cannot incur the loss of liberty or property for an offence by a judicial proceeding until he has had a fair opportunity of answering the charge against him, unless the Legislature has expressly or impliedly given an authority to act without that necessary preliminary."

It is then a question of deciding whether the requirement to give notice has been excluded either expressly or by necessary

Fines, costs, compensation and forfeited recognizances

implication. It has certainly not been expressly excluded. Whether the requirement has been excluded by necessary implication is a question which can perhaps be more properly answered elsewhere than in a magistrates' court and is one which can be easily avoided by the issue of a summons for the purpose of arrears proceedings.

The warrant must name or otherwise describe the person against whom the distress is to be levied. It must be directed to the constables of the police area in which the warrant is issued; or to the authorised persons for the police area specified in the warrant; or to a person named in the warrant. It requires such person to levy the outstanding sum by distress and sale of goods belonging to the person named (r 54 MCR 1981).

Form 48 in the Magistrates' Courts Forms Rules 1981 is the prescribed form of warrant of distress.

8. Crown Court fines

Any fine imposed or recognizance forfeited by the Crown Court is treated for the purposes of collection, enforcement and remission as having been imposed or forfeited by the magistrates' court specified in the order made by the Crown Court, or, if no such order is made, the magistrates' court by whom the offender was committed to be tried or dealt with. It must be noted, however, that a magistrates' court cannot remit (see page 16) any such fine or forfeited recognizance without first obtaining the consent of the Crown Court (s 32(1) Powers of Criminal Courts Act 1973).

On imposing a fine, the Crown Court may allow time for payment; order payment by instalments; or, in the case of a recognizance, discharge the same or reduce the amount thereunder (s 31(1) Powers of Criminal Courts Act 1973). The power to allow time for payment or to order payment by instalments also applies to costs and compensation.

Where the Crown Court has fixed a term of imprisonment to be served on default in payment, then the term to be specified in the warrant of commitment must be the term imposed by the Crown Court less any reduction for part-payment (s 32(2) Powers of Criminal Courts Act 1973).

9. Remission

Once a fine has been imposed, then, quite apart from any possible avenue of appeal, it does not necessarily mean that the fine stands forever, to be paid whatever the circumstances. In appropriate cases it is open to the court to consider ordering that the fine be reduced.

(a) Fines

The court has power to remit the whole or part of any fine imposed as it thinks just, but may do so only after inquiry into the offender's means (see page 3); or at a hearing with a view to the issue of a warrant of commitment, having had regard to any change in the offender's circumstances since the conviction. It is a matter for the discretion of the court, a discretion which should be exercised judicially and which, until now, has not been used as often as it could have been.

Where the court remits the whole or part of a fine after a term of imprisonment has been fixed, it must also reduce proportionately the term of imprisonment (s 85 MCA 1980).

It must be noted that the word "fine" used in this context does not include any other sum adjudged to be paid by conviction. There is no power, except that discussed below, to remit costs, compensation or a forfeited recognizance.

The consent of the Crown Court is required before the court can remit the whole or part of a fine imposed by the Crown Court.

These provisions are amended by s 6(5) Criminal Justice Act 1988 which, when in force, will replace s 85 MCA 1980 with a new section. Section 85 will in future provide that the court may at any time remit the whole or part of any fine where it is considered just to do so, either before or after the issue of a warrant of commitment, having regard to the change of circumstances since the date of conviction or the date when the warrant of commitment was first postponed or further postponed, or the conditions of the postponement varied, whichever is the later.

(b) Recognizances

Although it has been said that the power to remit a fine does not extend to the remission of a forfeited recognizance, a recognizance can be remitted by a different power contained in MCA 1980. By this, at any time before the issue of a warrant of commitment to enforce payment of the outstanding sum, or before the sale of goods under a warrant of distress to satisfy the outstanding sum, the court may remit the whole or any part of the sum either absolutely or on such conditions as the court thinks just (s 120(4) MCA 1980).

Fines, costs, compensation and forfeited recognizances

Where the court does remit, the provisions applicable to fines concerning proportionate reductions of any periods of imprisonment also apply.

(c) Compensation

Although compensation cannot be remitted under the provision relating to fines, an order for compensation can be reviewed with a view to its discharge or reduction.

An application to review must be made to the court responsible for enforcing the order, and must be made by the person against whom the order was made.

On such application if it appears to the court:

(i) that the injury, loss or damage in respect of which the order was made has been held in civil proceedings to be less than it was taken to be for the purposes of the order; or

(ii) in the case of an order in respect of the loss of any property, that the property has been recovered by the person in whose favour the order was made;

the court may discharge the order, or reduce the amount which remains to be paid (s 37 Powers of Criminal Courts Act 1973).

Section 105 CJA 1988, when in force, amends the enforcement provisions regarding compensation orders. New sections are substituted in the Powers of Criminal Courts Act 1973 to replace the existing ss 36 to 38. Under the new provisions, where a compensation order is made, the person in whose favour it is made is not entitled to payment until there is no further possibility of an appeal on which the order could be varied or set aside. Rules will make provision concerning the way in which magistrates' courts having power to enforce compensation orders are to deal with money paid while the entitlement is suspended.

When there is no longer any possibility of an appeal, the person ordered to pay the compensation may apply to a magistrates' court responsible for enforcing the order to reduce or discharge the order, providing the application is made before the full amount has been paid. The court may reduce or discharge the order where it appears:

(i) that the injury, loss or damage has been held in civil proceedings to be less than the order; or

(ii) in the case of an order for loss of property, that the property has been recovered; or

- (iii) that the means of the person against whom the order was made are insufficient to satisfy the order in full and a confiscation order (see page 42) has been made against him in the same proceedings; or
- (iv) that the person against whom the order was made has suffered a substantial reduction in his means which was unexpected at the time the compensation order was made, and that his means seem unlikely to increase for a considerable period.

Where the order was made by a Crown Court, a magistrates' court may not exercise the power in cases (iii) or (iv) above unless the consent of the Crown Court is first obtained.

10. Power to search

Where a court has adjudged a person to pay a sum by conviction the court may order him to be searched. Any money found on the defaulter may, unless the court otherwise directs, be applied towards payment of the outstanding sum (s 80 MCA 1980).

In addition, any money found on the arrest of such person, or on his being taken to a prison or other place of detention in default of payment, or for want of sufficient distress, may be applied towards payment of the outstanding sum.

The court must not, however, allow the application of any money found in this manner if it is satisfied that the money does not belong to the offender, or that the loss of money would be more injurious to his family than would be his detention.

11. Juveniles

No form of custodial order may be made in respect of a person under seventeen years of age (s 1 CJA 1982). However, where a court would, but for the statutory restrictions upon the imprisonment of young offenders, have power to commit to prison a person under the age of seventeen for default in payment, or for want of sufficient distress, the court may:

- (i) make an order requiring a parent or guardian to enter into a recognizance to ensure that the juvenile pays the amount due (s 81(1) MCA 9180). The parent or guardian must consent to such an order. If consent is not given, the parent or guardian cannot be committed to prison for

Fines, costs, compensation and forfeited recognizances

withholding that consent as in the case of a recognizance to keep the peace and be of good behaviour. In the absence of consent an order cannot be made;
(ii) make an order directing that the amount outstanding be paid by the parent or guardian instead (s 81(1)(b) MCA 1980).

The amount outstanding is then enforced in the same way as if the parent or guardian had been convicted of the offence (s 81(7) MCA 1980).

An order may only be made where the court is satisfied that the defaulter has, or has had since the conviction, the means to pay, and has refused or neglected to do so (s 81(5) MCA 1980). The parent or guardian must be given an opportunity of being heard before an order is made. An order under (ii) above can be made in the absence of a parent or guardian, who, having been required to attend, fails to do so (s 81(5) MCA 1980).

The importance of the above provisions must now be diminished in the light of s 26 Criminal Justice Act 1982 which requires that where a juvenile is convicted of an offence and is ordered to pay a fine, costs or compensation, it is the duty of the court to order that the amount ordered be paid by the parent or guardian, unless satisfied that the parent or guardian cannot be found or that it would be unreasonable to make such an order under all the circumstances.

12. Attendance centre orders

Where a court would have power, but for the statutory restriction upon imprisonment of persons under twenty-one years of age, to commit such person to prison in default of payment the court may instead make an attendance centre order for a specified number of hours, provided that an attendance centre is available and reasonably accessible to the offender, having regard to his age, the means of access available to him and any other circumstances (s 17(1) CJA 1981).

An order can be made before a previous order has ceased to have effect (s 17(6) CJA 1981). The court may determine the number of hours to be specified in the order without regard to the number specified in the previous order, or to the fact that the order is still in effect.

An order cannot be made in respect of a person who has previously been sentenced to imprisonment, borstal training, youth custody, or detention in a detention centre, unless it appears to the court that there are special circumstances (whether relating to the offence or to the offender) which warrant the making of such an order (s 17(3) CJA 1982).

Nor can an order be made in respect of a person under seventeen years of age for default in payment or for want of sufficient distress, unless the court has, since the conviction, inquired into his means in his presence on at least one occasion (see page 18) (s 81(3)(a) MCA 1980).

Form 38 in the Magistrates' Courts (Children and Young Persons) Rules 1988 is the prescribed form of order. See Appendix.

(b) Number of hours

No guidance is given about the number of hours to be imposed in relation to different sizes of fine, save that:

(i) the aggregate number of hours should not be less than twelve, except in relation to a child under fourteen, when the number of hours may be less than twelve if the court is of the opinion that twelve hours would be excessive having regard to the age of the child or any other circumstances;

(ii) the aggregate number of hours should not exceed twelve except where the court is of the opinion, having regard to all the circumstances, that twelve hours would be inadequate, in which case the aggregate number of hours should not exceed twenty-four where the offender is under seventeen years of age or thirty-six hours where the offender is under twenty-one but not less than seventeen

(s 17(4) and (5) CJA 1982).

(c) Service of orders

A copy of the order must be delivered or sent to the officer in charge of the attendance centre (s 17(12) CJA 1982). In addition, a copy must be delivered to the offender or sent by registered or recorded delivery post to the offender's last or usual place of abode.

Fines, costs, compensation and forfeited recognizances

(d) Payments received after order made

After an order has been made, payment of the whole sum will cause the order to cease to have effect (s 17(13) CJA 1982).

Payment of part only will mean that the total number of hours is reduced proportionately. For example, where twelve hours attendance were ordered for non-payment of £100, payment of £50 reduces the twelve hours to six.

Payment made be made either to the clerk of the court which made the order or to the officer in charge of the attendance centre (r 41 Magistrates' Courts (Children and Young Persons) Rules 1988). An officer at the attendance centre is not required to accept a part-payment unless it is an amount which will secure a reduction of one complete hour or multiple thereof. Where the clerk receives payment he must notify the officer in charge of the attendance centre.

(e) Failure to comply with an order

In the event of failure to comply with an attendance centre order the court may revoke the order and deal with the defaulter in any way in which the court could have done so originally for default in payment. It follows that a fresh order can be made and the alternative methods of enforcing payment may be used, including commitment in default except in relation to persons under seventeen.

13. Enforcement by High Court and county court

If all else fails the clerk of a magistrates' court may take proceedings in the High Court or county court to recover an outstanding sum, but only after he has been duly authorised by a magistrates' court following an inquiry into the defendant's means (see page 3).

Proceedings may be taken in regard to any sum adjudged to be paid by a conviction of a magistrates' court as if in pursuance of a judgment or order of the High Court or county court. Proceedings will be taken in either the High Court or county court according to the size of the outstanding sum. If it exceeds the financial jurisdiction of the county court (£5,000 at May 1988), proceedings should instead be brought in the High Court.

The remedies available in the High Court or county court are limited to proceedings for the attachment of debts owed to the defendant; garnishee proceedings; and the making of an order charging the defendant's land or a receiver by way of equitable execution. A writ of *fieri facias* or other process against goods is excluded as is imprisonment and attachment of earnings since these are remedies available in the magistrates' court.

The procedure in the High Court is governed by Rules of the Supreme Court OO 49, 50 and 51 and in the county court by County Court Rules OO 25, 27, 30 and 31.

It is for the justices' clerk to take the proceedings, which are made *ex parte* supported by affidavit. In the case of garnishee proceedings the name of the debtor must be set out together with the amount of the debt if this is known. In special circumstances, however, a receiver may be appointed by way of equitable execution in lieu of garnishee proceedings, for example, where the existence of debts is not known and there is no way of finding out (*Goldshmidt* v *Oberrheinische Metallwerke* (1906)).

14. Recording details of enforcement

An entry must be made in a register kept by the court, or any separate record kept for the purpose of recording particulars, of any of the following:

- (a) a means inquiry;
- (b) a hearing with a view to committal;
- (c) allowance of further time to pay;
- (d) a direction to pay by instalments;
- (e) distress for enforcement;
- (f) attachment of earnings;
- (g) supervision pending payment;
- (h) an order remitting the whole or part of any fine;
- (i) an order remitting the whole or part of any forfeited recognizance;
- (j) authority granted for the taking of proceedings in the High Court or county court for the recovery of the sum outstanding;
- (k) a transfer of fine order made by the court;
- (l) an order transferring a fine to the court;
- (m) an order from the Crown Court specifying the court as the appropriate court to enforce a fine imposed or recognizance forfeited by the Crown Court;

(n) any fine imposed or recognizance forfeited by a coroner that has to be treated as having been imposed or forfeited by the court

(r 65(2) MCR 1981).

In addition, where at the time of conviction a warrant of commitment is issued, or a term of imprisonment fixed and the issue of the warrant of commitment postponed in respect of default in payment, the reasons for the court's action must be entered in the register (r 65(1) MCR 1981).

15. The Channel Islands and the Isle of Man

To date the various statutory enforcement provisions which are available in England and Wales, Scotland and Northern Ireland have not been extended to the Channel Islands or the Isle of Man. Steps cannot therefore be taken against anyone living there.

16. Financial penalty enforcement orders — armed forces

On entering the armed forces, a serviceman becomes subject to a code of naval, military or air force law, and various disciplinary provisions apply. While in the forces it is possible that a financial penalty may be ordered against a serviceman for an offence. Where this is so in relation to what is called a "qualifying offence", and the serviceman leaves the forces and is no longer subject to service law, the Defence Council (the authority responsible for exercising on behalf of the Crown the powers of command and administration over the armed forces) or a person authorised on behalf of the Defence Council, may make a financial penalty enforcement order in respect of the outstanding sum. The order is then sent for registration in the magistrates' court acting for the area within whose jurisdiction the person against whom the order is made appears to reside or is likely to reside (s 133A(1) Army Act 1955; s 133A Air Force Act 1955; s 128F(1) Naval Discipline Act 1957).

The order will contain a certificate setting out details of the penalty and outstanding sum. Rule 47 MCA 1981 requires the clerk of a magistrates' court receiving such an order to register the order by means of a memorandum entered in the court register and to send written notice to the Defence Council or authorised officer stating that the order has been registered. Once the order is registered the clerk must serve notice of the registration on the person against whom the order was made. The prescribed form of notice is in

Form 47 Magistrates' Courts (Forms) Rules 1981, and may be served by delivering it to the person or by sending it by post addressed to him at the address shown on the financial penalty enforcement order. Once the order is registered service enforcement procedures cease to be available for recovery of the outstanding sum and the penalty is enforced as if it were a fine imposed on conviction by the relevant magistrates' court.

17. Fines imposed by coroners

A fine imposed by a coroner, or a recognizance forfeited at an inquest heard before a coroner, is to be treated for the purposes of collection, enforcement and remission as having been imposed by the magistrates' court for the area in which the coroner's court was held.

The coroner is required to give particulars of the fine to the clerk to the justices as soon as is practicable after the fine has been imposed (s 67 CJA 1988, now in force).

18. Fines on companies

Section 62 CJA 1988 will, when in force, add s 87A to the MCA 1980. The new section enables a clerk to a magistrates' court to take civil proceedings against a company in respect of any sum adjudged to be paid by a conviction where a distress warrant has been issued and the warrant is returned because of insufficient distress. The clerk may apply for an administration order under s 9 Insolvency Act 1986. An administration order directs that while the order is in force, the affairs, business and property of the company should be arranged by a person, called the administrator, appointed by the court for the purpose.

The clerk may also petition for the winding-up of the company under s 124 of the same Act.

In either case there is no requirement that the clerk be first authorised by a magistrates' court to take the proceedings.

19. Civilian enforcement officers

Section 65 CJA 1988 adds subs 2 to s 125 MCA 1980. This provision authorises civilian enforcement officers to execute warrants of arrest, warrants of commitment and warrants of distress for non-payment of a fine. Section 136(2)(a) of the Act is also amended to permit a civilian enforcement officer to execute a warrant for the detention of a fine defaulter overnight in a police station.

Chapter 2

Imprisonment and detention

1. Introduction

Although the court has power to order imprisonment, subject to certain conditions (s 76 MCA 1980), it is a step which should not be taken lightly. There are other methods of enforcement which can and must be considered first. Indeed in *R* v *Birmingham Justices, ex parte Bennett* (1983) it was said that should there be a reasonable likelihood that the defendant has assets available to satisfy the sum he owes, magistrates should proceed by way of a warrant of distress rather than by committing him to prison. Although the case concerned only costs and compensation, it is submitted that the approach is equally valid for fines.

Once the stage has been reached where there is no alternative but to impose imprisonment the court should seek to impose the shortest possible term which can adequately deal with the situation. The periods of imprisonment which may be imposed are contained in Sch 4 MCA 1980 (see below) and vary according to the amount outstanding. It is of the greatest importance to recognise that the terms of imprisonment are expressed as maxima. Courts should adopt a flexible approach and impose shorter periods where circumstances permit. Among the matters which the court should take into account may be that defaulter has never been in prison before; or that the fine was imposed for an offence which does not carry imprisonment as a penalty.

The maximum periods of imprisonment which may be imposed in the event of non-payment are as follows. The right hand column shows reduced periods of imprisonment for amounts not over £10,000, set out in s 60 CJA 1988:

Imprisonment and detention

Amount unpaid Exceeding—but not exceeding		Maximum term	Max term under CJ Act 1988
	£50	7 days	5 days
£50	£100	14 days	7 days
£100	£400	30 days	14 days
£400	£1,000	60 days	30 days
£1,000	£2,000	90 days	45 days
£2,000	£5,000	6 months	3 months
£5,000	£10,000	9 months	6 months
£10,000		12 months	

(Sch 4 MCA 1980).

2. Consecutive periods of imprisonment

Consecutive periods of imprisonment may be imposed subject to a maximum period of six months. Where, however, two or more periods of imprisonment are imposed for non-payment of fines, in respect of offences triable either way, the aggregate of the terms so imposed may exceed six months but must not exceed twelve months. The limitation does not operate to reduce the aggregate of the terms which may be imposed below that which could be imposed in respect of any one of the outstanding sums (s 133 MCR 1980).

Should the court wish to impose consecutive terms of imprisonment in regard to a number of outstanding fines, and the aggregate period of imprisonment to be imposed exceeds that which could have been imposed had the total of the individual fines been imposed as one single amount, then separate warrants of commitment must be issued. To impose consecutive periods of imprisonment, it is not sufficient to use a single warrant setting out details of different periods of imprisonment. All that will achieve is that the aggregate period of imprisonment will be reduced to that applicable to the totalled sum of the outstanding fines. This is the effect of two High Court decisions: *R v Southampton Justices, ex parte Davies* (1981) and *R v Midhurst Justices, ex parte Seymour* (1983).

In *Seymour* the court outlined the approach to be followed by justices; they must look at the whole of the circumstances, including the offences for which the fines were imposed and the amounts sought to be enforced. If satisfied that justice could be done by imposing a term not exceeding the statutory maximum, it is appropriate to do so on a single sheet. If, after full consideration, it is felt right that the aggregate of sentences imposed should exceed the maximum, separate warrants in respect of each committal should be issued.

3. Postponement of issue of warrant

On imposing imprisonment or detention in respect of an outstanding fine, the court may, if it thinks it expedient to do so, fix the term of imprisonment or detention and postpone the issue of the warrant of commitment until such time and upon such conditions, if any, as the court thinks just (s 77(2) MCA 1980). Whether it is expedient to postpone the issue of the warrant is a matter for the courts to decide.

It had been accepted for some time that once a magistrates' court has exercised its powers under s 77(2) MCA 1980, to fix a term of imprisonment or detention and postpone the issue of the warrant of commitment, thereafter no power existed to review the terms of the postponement in the event of further default or a change in circumstances. In *R* v *Colchester Justices, ex parte Wilson* (1985) it was held by the House of Lords that this is no longer the case. The House of Lords said that a magistrates' court could indeed exercise the power contained in s 77(2) as often as the justices considered appropriate. Lord Roskill said that :

> "...there was no reason why the powers given by s 77(2) should not be exercised from time to time and indeed as often as the justices concerned considered that the occasion required. So to hold was not to encourage or facilitate deliberate and inexcusable default: no doubt courts would be alert to see that the existence of the power further to postpone was not abused but was only exercised as the occasion required".

Of earlier cases in which it had been held that the power did not exist it was said that they had been wrongly decided. The decision, however, goes further than merely stating that a magistrates' court may vary the terms of a postponed commitment. Their Lordships referred to the requirements of natural justice and to the comments of Lord Fraser in *Forrest* v *Brighton Justices* (1981). The effect of this seems to be that where default is made in the terms of a postponed commitment then before any warrant is issued a hearing must take place at which the defendant has the opportunity to attend to make representations. It seems to follow that the same applies equally to the question of the issue of distress

Imprisonment and detention

warrants. The *Colchester Justices* case follows that of *Forrest v Brighton Justices* (see page 14). Section 61(1) CJA 1988 will, when in force, put these decisions into statutory form. Section 77(2) MCA 1980 is amended by the addition of a number of subsections, so that where the issue of a warrant of commitment is postponed, the court may subsequently vary the terms of postponement where it is just to do so, having regard to a change of circumstances since the issue of the warrant was first postponed, or the terms of postponement last varied.

The person in respect of whom the issue of the warrant has been postponed may apply to a justice of the peace acting for the petty sessions area in which the warrant has been or would be issued, with a view to the court exercising this power. If it appears to the justice that there has been a change in circumstances which would make it just for the courts to exercise the power of variation, the justice must refer the matter to the court. The clerk of the court must then arrange the date of the hearing and give the applicant notice. Furthermore, where a warrant of commitment has already been issued before the hearing of the application, the court has power to order that the warrant shall cease to have effect,

4. Imprisonment at time of conviction

The court may order imprisonment at the same time as it convicts for the offence if, but only if:

(a) the offence is punishable with imprisonment and the offender appears to the court to have sufficient means to pay the sum forthwith; or

(b) it appears to the court that the offender is unlikely to remain long enough at a place of abode in the United Kingdom to enable payment to be enforced by other method; or

(c) the court sentences the offender to immediate imprisonment, youth custody or detention for the offence itself, or the offender is already serving a sentence of custody for life, or a term of imprisonment, youth custody, or detention under s 9 CJA 1982, or detention in a detention centre (s 82(1) MCA 1980).

The court may not, at the time of conviction, fix a term of imprisonment to be served in the event of future default in payment unless:

(a) the court has power to impose imprisonment forthwith; and
(b) the court exercises the power to postpone the issue of the warrant of commitment
(s 82(2) MCA 1980).

See page 137 for the prescribed form of warrant of commitment.

5. Imprisonment on occasion after conviction

Where imprisonment in default of payment is not imposed at the time of conviction, it may be imposed later if, but only if:

(a) the defaulter is already serving a term of imprisonment or detention; or
(b) the court has, since the conviction, inquired into his means in his presence on at least one occasion (see below)
(s 82(3) MCA 1980).

See page 138 for the prescribed form of warrant of commitment.

6. Means inquiry

(a) Generally

Where the court inquires into the means of a defaulter (see page 3), it may not, on that occasion or at any time thereafter, impose imprisonment for default unless:

(i) the offence to which the sum relates is punishable with imprisonment, and the defaulter appears to the court to have sufficient means to pay the sum forthwith; or
(ii) the court is satisfied that the default is due to the offender's wilful refusal or culpable neglect, and the court has considered or tried all other methods of enforcing payment and it appears to the court that they are inappropriate or unsuccessful
(s 82(4) MCA 1980).

Section 61(3) CJA 1988, when in force, will insert subsection 4A into s 82 MCA 1980 and provides that the methods of enforcing payment mentioned at (ii) above are:

(i) a warrant of distress (see page 10);

Imprisonment and detention

    (ii)   an application by the clerk to the justices to the High Court or county court for enforcement (see page 21);
    (ii)   a money payments supervision order (see page 8);
    (iv)   an attachment of earnings order (see page 91);
    (v)   an attendance centre order (see page 19).

In *R* v *Norwich Magistrates' Court, ex parte Tigger (formerly Lilly)* (1987), a magistrates' court had inquired into an offender's means and satisfied itself that the default in payment was due to wilful refusal or culpable neglect, but had not, on the evidence, discharged its duty to consider or try all other methods of enforcement before issuing a warrant of commitment. The committal warrants were therefore quashed. It was also held that, when considering the means of a defendant, it is incumbent upon the justices to ascertain whether the prosecution still hold any assets belonging to him. In *R* v *Clacton Justices and Another, ex parte Commissioners of Customs and Excise* (1987) a fine of £10,000 was owing, but unbeknown to the justices, some £20,000 was still in the possession of the prosecution. The Court of Appeal held that it was quite plain, on the authority of *R* v *Birmingham Justices ex parte Bennett* (1983), that the justices had failed properly to exercise their discretion when issuing the warrant of commitment, in not considering the defendant's means and ascertaining whether the prosecution held any of his assets.

Where a court intends to issue a warrant of commitment, the offender must be present, unless:

    (a)   the court has previously fixed a term of imprisonment and postponed the issue of the warrant; or
    (b)   the offender is already serving a term of imprisonment or detention. Although the court may impose imprisonment for default in the offender's absence if he is already serving imprisonment or detention, this does not mean that the court may dispense with a hearing before the warrant of commitment is issued. There must be a hearing and notice of it must be given to the offender, affording him an opportunity of being heard (*Forrest* v *Brighton Justices* (1981)).

Section 61(4) CJA 1988, when in force, will amend s 82 MCA 1980 by the addition of subs 5A and supplementary subsections, whereby a magistrates' court may not issue a warrant of commitment at a hearing at which the offender is not present unless the clerk of the court has served notice on the offender that the court intends to hold a hearing to consider whether to issue the warrant, and stating the reason why. The date and time of the hearing must be contained in the notice and must not be earlier than twenty-one days after the issue of the notice, unless at the same time as the court exercises the power to impose imprisonment and postpones the issue of the warrant, a notice of intended hearing is issued, in which case the hearing may be held at any time after the end of the period for which the issue of the warrant has been postponed, which could be less than 21 days.

(b) Power to secure attendance at means inquiry

For the purpose of securing the attendance of an offender at a means inquiry the court may:

    (i)   issue a summons requiring his attendance; or
    (ii)   issue a warrant for his arrest
        (s 83 MCA 1980).

If the offender fails to appear, the court may issue a warrant for his arrest. Any warrant so issued ceases to have effect when the outstanding sum is paid to the police officer holding the warrant. See pages 139 and 140 for the prescribed forms of summons and warrant.

(c) Power to require statement of means

Section 84 MCA 1980 provides that the court may order an offender to furnish, within a specified period, such statement of means as the court may require (s 84 MCA 1980). The statement of means may be ordered to be given either before, or upon, inquiring into a person's means. An order made before an inquiry can be made by a single justice or justices' clerk. Failure to comply with such an order will render a person liable on summary conviction to a fine not exceeding Level 3 on the standard scale (s 37 CJA 1982 and s 84(2) MCA 1980).

If a statement furnished in accordance with such an order is known to the maker to be false in a material particular; or is made recklessly and is false in a material particular; or the maker knowingly fails to disclose any material fact; the maker of the statement is liable on summary conviction to a term of imprisonment not exceeding four months, or a fine not exceeding Level 3 on the standard scale or both (s 84(3) MCA 1980).

7. Reduction of period of imprisonment

Where imprisonment has been imposed for default of payment, payment of the outstanding sum will cause the order to cease to have effect and, if a person is in custody, he must be released

Imprisonment and detention

unless he is in custody for some other reason (s 79(1) MCA 1980). Payment of part only of the outstanding sum will reduce, but not erase, the period of imprisonment. Part payment may take place either before or after imprisonment is imposed. The effect on reducing the period of imprisonment is different in each case.

(a) Part-payment before imprisonment imposed

Where part-payment is made before imprisonment is imposed, the maximum period of imprisonment which may be imposed in relation to the balance outstanding is that applicable to the original sum, reduced by such number of days as bears to the total number of days the same proportion as the part-payment bears to the whole sum (para 2(1) MCA 1980 Sch 4).

Any fraction of a day is left out of account, and the period must not be reduced to less than five days (Sch 4 para 2(2) MCA 1980). For example, X is originally fined £45 and £15 costs, making a total of £60. He would therefore be liable to fourteen days imprisonment in default. X pays £15 before the means inquiry, leaving a balance of £45 — three quarters of the total. To reduce the fourteen days in proportion to the amount paid (one quarter of the total), it is necessary to deduct one quarter of fourteen days — ie three and a half days. But in calculating the reduction, fractions of a day are omitted. Therefore the committal will be for eleven days (14 minus 3).

(b) Part-payment after imprisonment imposed

Where part-payment is made *after* imprisonment has been imposed, the period of imprisonment is reduced by such number of days as bears to the total number of days imposed, less one day, the same proportion as the part-payment bears to the amount outstanding at the time imprisonment was imposed. In making the necessary reduction, any fraction of a day must not be taken into account. For example, X being in default of payment of the balance of £45 is committed to eleven days' imprisonment in default, suspended on terms. He has paid only £5 since and the period of imprisonment is reduced by :

$$\frac{£5 \times 10 \text{ days} [11-1]}{£45} = 1\ ^{1/9} \text{ days}$$

Again fractions of days are omitted and the committal will be for 10 days (11–1).

The period of imprisonment in this case is capable of being reduced to a period of less than five days, and r 55(5) MCR 1981 provides that where a period of imprisonment is so reduced through part payment, a person may be committed either to a prison or to a place certified by the Secretary of State to be suitable for the purpose for a period not exceeding four days. Police cells may be certified as being so suitable. (Rule 55(5) does not apply in a case where detention has been ordered on a person under twenty-one years of age).

This provision would at first sight appear to conflict with s 132 MCA 1980, which provides that a magistrates' court may not impose imprisonment for a period of less than five days. But the wording of s 132 is important. It refers to the act of imposing imprisonment and not to the act of issuing a warrant of commitment after imprisonment has been imposed. Where s 55(5) MCR 1981 applies, the court has already imposed imprisonment before any reduction for part-payment is taken into account. The warrant of commitment therefore contains the number of days imposed, less any reduction for part-payment. This may then result in a person being committed to prison for less than five days.

8. Receipt of payments after imprisonment imposed

The persons authorised to receive payment or part-payment after imprisonment has been imposed are as follows:

(a) unless a warrant of commitment has been issued, the clerk of the enforcing court or supervisor appointed under a fine supervision order;
(b) any constable holding the warrant of commitment;
(c) the governor or keeper of the prison or place in which the offender is detained
(r 55 MCR 1981).

9. Detention for short periods

(a) Detention in a place certified by the Secretary of State

Where the court has power to impose imprisonment for default in payment, it may instead order an offender to be detained for any period not exceeding four days in a place certified by the Secretary of State to be suitable for the purpose (s 134(1) MCA 1980). The court cannot, however, make such an order for default in payment in the case of a person under twenty-one years of age (s 134(8) MCA 1980). A check can be made with the local chief officer of police as to whether police cells are certified. See page 141 for the prescribed form of warrant for detention. Note that s 134 MCA 1980 will be repealed by Sch 16 CJA 1988 when in force.

(b) Detention for one day in court house or police station

Where the court has power, or would have power, to impose imprisonment or detention for default in payment but for the statutory restrictions relating to such imprisonment or detention, the court may instead order a person to be detained within the precincts of the court-house or at any police station until such hour, not later than 8 o'clock in the evening of the day on which the order is made, as the court may direct. If it does so, it must not commit to prison or order detention in default (s 135 MCA 1980). It is not necessary to allow time for payment or hold a means inquiry. Nor need any of the other restrictions relating to imprisonment or detention in default of payment be complied with. This provision cannot be used in regard to a person under seventeen years of age.

(c) Detention overnight at police station

Here, as above, the court may, instead of imposing imprisonment or detention in default of payment, issue a warrant for the detention of an offender in a police station (s 136 MCA 1980). The restrictions that relate to the imposition of imprisonment or detention in default of payment do not apply. See page 142 for the prescribed form of warrant of detention.

A warrant issued for such detention authorises any police constable to arrest the offender and take him to a police station, and requires that the offender be detained until 8 o'clock on the morning of the day following that on which he is arrested, or if he is arrested between midnight and 8 o'clock in the morning, until 8 o'clock in the morning of the day on which he is arrested. The officer in charge of the station may, however, release the offender at any time within four hours before 8 o'clock in the morning if he thinks it expedient to do so, to enable the offender to go to work, or for any other reason appearing to the officer to be sufficient. This provision does not apply to persons under seventeen years of age. (s 136(3) MCA 1980.)

10. Execution in different parts of the United Kingdom of warrants for imprisonment for non-payment of fine

(a) Scotland

A warrant issued in England and Wales, committing a person to prison for non-payment of fine, may be executed in Scotland by any constable appointed for a police area, as if the warrant were an extract conviction for imprisonment issued in Scotland in default of payment of the fine (s 38(A) Criminal Law Act 1977). A person arrested by virtue of this provision can be detained in any prison in Scotland, and while he is so detained he is to be treated for all purposes as if he were detained under an extract conviction issued in Scotland. Execution of the warrant may take place whether or not it has been endorsed under s 4 of the Summary Jurisdiction (Process) Act 1981.

(b) Northern Ireland

A warrant issued in England and Wales, committing a person to prison for non-payment of a fine, may be executed in Northern Ireland by a member of the Royal Ulster Constabulary as if the warrant were a warrant committing him to prison in default of payment of a sum adjudged to be paid by a conviction in Northern Ireland (s 38(B) Criminal Law Act 1977). A person arrested by virtue of this provision may be detained in any prison in Northern Ireland, and while he is so detained he is to be treated for all purposes as if he were detained under a warrant of commitment issued in Northern Ireland.

(c) England and Wales

Similar provisions exist for the execution in England and Wales of warrants of commitment for non-payment of fine issued in Scotland and Northern Ireland.

11. Young persons

(a) Detention

No form of custodial order may be made in respect of a person under seventeen years of age.

A term of imprisonment may not be imposed on a person under twenty-one years of age. However, where but for this restriction a court would have power to commit a person under twenty-one but not less than seventeen years of age for default in payment, it may instead commit him to be detained or make an order fixing a term

Imprisonment and detention

of detention in the event of default, for a term not exceeding the term of imprisonment (ss 1 and 9 CJA 1982). Before the court may commit a person to be detained as above:

(i) the conditions required to be satisfied before imprisonment can be imposed for default in payment must be satisfied (see below);

(ii) the court must be of the opinion that no other method of dealing with the offender is appropriate (s 1(5) CJA 1982);

(iii) where the court does commit to detention for default in payment it must state in open court the reason for its opinion that no other method of dealing with the offender is appropriate (s 2(5) CJA 1982). Any reason stated in accordance with this requirement must be specified in the warrant of commitment and entered in the register (s 2(7) CJA 1982).

Although there is no requirement that the court must obtain a social inquiry report for the purpose of determining whether there is any other appropriate method of dealing with such a person, it must obtain and consider information about the circumstances, and take into account any information before it which is relevant to the person's character and his physical and mental condition (s 2(1) CJA 1982).

An order that a person be detained in accordance with the above provisions is an order that a person be detained:

(i) in a remand centre;

(ii) in a detention centre (young offenders institution under CJA 1988);

(iii) in a youth custody centre (young offenders institution under CJA 1988); or

(iv) in any place in which a person aged twenty-one years or over could be imprisoned or detained for default in payment of a fine or any other sum of money, as the Secretary of State may from time to time direct (s 12(10) CJA 1982.

See page 137 for the prescribed form of warrant of commitment. The issue of the warrant of commitment may be postponed in the same way as in the case of imprisonment (s 77(2) MCA 1980; see page 28). Any reduction in the period of detention as a result of any part-payment is calculated in the same way as in the case of imprisonment (see above).

Where an offender is already serving a sentence of detention or youth custody, a period of detention in default of payment may be imposed under the same conditions as apply in the case of imprisonment.

(b) Consecutive periods of detention

There is no direct statutory authority to the effect that consecutive periods of detention for default in payment may be imposed. It is therefore necessary to consider a number of different statutory provisions.

The general power to impose imprisonment in default is contained in s 76 MCA 1980, extended by s 133 to include power to impose consecutive periods of imprisonment. Section 1 CJA 1982 prohibits entirely imprisonment for the under twenty-one year olds. The power to impose imprisonment for default and thereby the power to impose consecutive periods of imprisonment are expressly excluded.

However, s 9 CJA 1982 goes on to provide that where, but for this prohibition, imprisonment in default could be imposed, then detention may be imposed for a term not exceeding the term of imprisonment. Thus, as the term of imprisonment which may be imposed for default could comprise several consecutive periods of imprisonment, it is submitted that consecutive periods of detention may also be imposed so as not to exceed the overall term of imprisonment which could otherwise be imposed. It is further submitted that it was the intention of Parliament to replace the method of incarceration rather than to affect the basic jurisdiction.

Chapter 3

Confiscation orders

1. Drug trafficking

(a) Power to make an order

The Drug Trafficking Offences Act 1986 requires the Crown Court, on convicting an offender of a drug trafficking offence (defined in s 38 of the Act), to make a confiscation order where appropriate. This means that before passing sentence, the Crown Court must determine whether, and to what extent, the convicted person has benefited from drug trafficking carried on by himself or another by receiving any payment or other reward.

The amount to which a person will be held to have benefited is determined in accordance with the provisions of s 4 of the Act. Once an amount is determined, the Crown Court must order the defendant to pay that sum. The sum ordered is referred to as a confiscation order and is enforced by a magistrates' court in the same way as a fine ordered by the Crown Court, subject to the following modifications:

(i) The periods of imprisonment imposed by the Crown Court in the event of default for amounts exceeding £10,000 are:

an amount exceeding £10,000 but not exceeding £20,000	12 months
an amount exceeding £20,000 but not exceeding £50,000	18 months
an amount exceeding £50,000 but not exceeding £100,000	2 years
an amount exceeding £100,000 but not exceeding £250,000	3 years
an amount exceeding £250,000 but not exceeding £1 million	5 years
an amount exceeding £1 million	10 years

In the magistrates' court any warrant of commitment issued for non-payment of a confiscation order must run consecutively with any period of imprisonment, youth custody or detention which the accused is serving in respect of the original drug trafficking offence or offences, including imprisonment or detention in default of payment of a fine imposed by the Crown Court for the offence or offences, except where the warrant of commitment for non-payment has not then been issued.

(ii) The amount ordered cannot be remitted as in the case of fines. However, the party liable to make payment can apply to the Crown Court for the amount ordered to be reduced, having first obtained the authority of the High Court (see further s 14).

(iii) In the case of persons under seventeen years of age, the court cannot make an order that a parent or guardian should enter a recognizance to ensure payment or directing that the parent or guardian pay the balance of the outstanding sum.

(iv) A means inquiry is not required before enforcement proceedings can be taken by the justices' clerk in the High Court.

Although a confiscation order is enforced in the same way as a fine, subject to the above modifications, a cautious approach is required. Unlike other outstanding sums, the prosecution may itself take enforcement action. A prosecutor may apply to the High Court for a restraining order prohibiting any person from dealing with any realisable property; and for the appointment of a receiver. Such action is quite separate and apart from enforcement action in the magistrates' court and any proceedings a justices' clerk may himself take in the High Court. In view of this, it is suggested, and urged by the Home Office, that there should at all times be liaison with the prosecution before any steps to enforce are taken in the magistrates' court.

(b) Application of sums received

In consequence of proceedings in the High Court by the prosecutor, payment may be made by a receiver to a justices' clerk. Where this is so the entire amount in the hands of the receiver is the amount to be taken as extinguishing or reducing the defendant's liability, less such payments (if any) as the High Court may direct. The justices' clerk must then apply the sum he receives firstly in payment of the receiver's remuneration and expenses, next in repaying a prosecutor for payments made by him to a receiver, the balance then to be remitted to the Secretary of State. Where payments are made otherwise than by a receiver appointed on the application of a prosecutor, the justices' clerk must treat the full amount received as operating to extinguish the debt, but must apply the sum received first in repaying a prosecutor for any payments made by him to a receiver.

The way in which a justices' clerk's accounts are credited will mean that when a payment is made by a receiver or from any other source, the justices' clerk must receipt the entire amount against the debit already raised in the cash book. He must then make an adjustment in the cash book to allow payment to be made to the various parties so as not to cause an imbalance in the accounts.

Schedule 5 para 6(1) CJA 1988 will, when in force, amend the order of priority by providing that where a sum is paid other than by a receiver the amount received by the justices' clerk must first be applied in paying the expenses of an insolvency practitioner before payments are made to reimburse a prosecutor for payments made to a receiver. As before, the entire amount received by the justices' clerk is the amount to be taken as extinguishing or reducing the liability.

(c) Imprisonment

Where default is made in payment of the outstanding sum and imprisonment for default has been imposed by the Crown Court, the warrant of commitment falls to be issued. A hearing must be held at which the defendant is given the opportunity to make representations and to put forward reasons why the warrant should not be issued. At the time the confiscation order was made, the Crown Court will have assessed the value of any assets available to satisfy the outstanding sum. The defendant may argue that the property is no longer capable of realising the value originally fixed and that is the reason for the failure to pay. In such a case the defendant should be given the opportunity to apply to the Crown Court for variation of the confiscation order.

2. Other powers to make confiscation orders

(a) The Criminal Justice Act 1988

Section 71 CJA 1988 will, when in force, give to Crown Courts and magistrates' courts the power to make confiscation orders in cases other than drug trafficking, requiring an offender to pay such sum as the court thinks fit. Where a person is convicted in the Crown

Court of an indictable offence which is not a drug trafficking offence, or is convicted by the Crown Court or a magistrates' court of an offence listed in Sch 4 (offences concerning sex establishments; supplying video recordings of unclassified work, or possessing for the purposes of supply; use of unlicensed premises for exhibition which require a licence) and the court is satisfied that he has benefited from the offence, and the benefit is at least £10,000, then, in addition to dealing with the offender in any other way, a confiscation order may be made for the sum to be paid. The sum ordered must be at least £10,000.

For the purposes of the Act a person is treated as having benefited from an offence if he obtains property or a pecuniary advantage as a result of or in connection with the commission of the offence. The benefit is then the value of the property or pecuniary advantage so obtained. The method of assessment is set out in the Act. No order can be made at all unless the prosecutor has given written notice to the court that it appears that were the court to consider making an order it would be able to make the offender pay at least the minimum sum. Unlike drug trafficking cases, the court has a discretion whether to make an order and is not duty bound to do so.

Furthermore, where the court makes both a confiscation order and at the same time an order for the payment of compensation and it appears that the defendant will not have sufficient means to satisfy both orders in full the court must direct that the compensation is paid out of any sums received under the confiscation order.

(b) Enforcement

Subject to the modifications shown below, a confiscation order made by the Crown Court is collected and enforced in a magistrates' court as if it were a fine imposed by the Crown Court. A confiscation order made by a magistrates' court is enforced as if it were a fine imposed by that court (s 75 CJA 1988, when in force).

As with confiscation orders in drug trafficking cases, a warrant of commitment issued by a magistrates' court must run consecutively with any period of imprisonment, youth custody or detention which the accused is then serving in respect of the original offence, including imprisonment or detention in default of payment of a fine for the offence, except where the Crown Court has imposed imprisonment or detention in default of payment of a fine and the warrant of commitment has not been issued.

The amount ordered may not be remitted as if it were a fine. The

Confiscation orders

defendant may, however, apply to the High Court for a certificate that realisable property is inadequate for the payment of the amount to be recovered under the order. He may then apply to the court which made the order for the amount to be reduced.

In the case of persons under seventeen years of age the court cannot make an order requiring a parent or guardian to enter a recognizance to ensure payment or directing a parent or guardian to pay the balance of the outstanding sum.

A means inquiry is not required before enforcement proceedings can be taken by the justices' clerk in the High Court.

As with drug trafficking offences, the prosecutor may take proceedings in the High Court for a restraining order, charging order and for the appointment of a receiver.

(c) Application of sums received

Sums in the hands of a receiver appointed in proceedings taken by the prosecutor are applied first in payment of expenses incurred (if any) by an insolvency practitioner (defined in s 388 Insolvency Act 1986); then to such payments if any as the High Court may direct; and thereafter in satisfaction of the debt. The justices' clerk receiving payment from a receiver must treat the full amount paid to him as operating to extinguish the outstanding debt, but must pay out of the sum received the expenses of the receiver before sending the balance to the Secretary of State.

Where the amount received by the justices' clerk is paid other than by a receiver, the justices' clerk must treat the full amount as reducing the sum payable, but then must pay the expenses of any insolvency practitioner; the prosecutor for any costs paid by him to a receiver; any compensation directed to be paid out of sums recovered under a confiscation order; and then and only then may the balance be remitted to the Secretary of State. A further complexity is that where a sum recovered under a confiscation order is to be applied in payment of a compensation order as well as remuneration and expenses, the person entitled to the compensation (the compensatee) is liable to pay a contribution out of the compensation towards the remuneration or expenses in the same proportion as the total amount of the compensation bears to the total amount of the confiscation order. The justices' clerk is then required to deduct this amount from the compensation which would otherwise be paid to the compensatee and the compensatee is treated as having received the full amount due.

Chapter 4

Fixed penalties

1. Introduction

On 1 October 1986 Part III of the Transport Act 1982 ("TA 1982") came into force, bringing with it a dramatic extension of the original 1960 fixed penalty system. Covering a much wider range of offences, the new system provides for a relatively low-cost and simple method of penalising road traffic offenders. Since there is no prosecution or court hearing the theory is that both police forces and magistrates' courts benefit; and of course those motorists who do pay also benefit by paying less as a result of waiving their right to a court hearing.

Where the motorist does not pay the penalty or request a hearing before the end of the "suspended enforcement period" (currently 28 days) the police must take further action to enforce the ticket through their central ticket office. This is done by a system of "fine registration". The motorist's lack of response to a notice served upon him raises a presumption of guilt of the original fixed penalty offence, and the Act then provides for the offence to be registered in the defaulter's home court for enforcement as a fine without a court hearing. This of course represents a major and radical departure from the accepted judicial practice in this country, and, recognising that mistakes can occur, certain safeguards have been built into the system to allow a defendant to challenge payment of the penalty and so avoid the consequences of enforcement.

2. Registration of sums payable in default for enforcement as fines

(a) Driver present

Where on the occasion of the offence a constable gives a fixed penalty notice to the person whom he believes to be the alleged offender and:

Fixed penalties

    (i)   the recipient does not give notice requesting a hearing; and
    (ii)   the fixed penalty is not paid before the end of the suspended enforcement period,

a sum equal to the fixed penalty plus one half of that amount may be registered for enforcement as a fine against the recipient of the notice (s 30(3) TA 1982).

(b) Driver not present

Where the fixed penalty notice has been affixed to a vehicle under s 27(2) TA 1982, if the penalty is not paid before the expiration of the suspended enforcement period and there is no request for a court hearing, the police may serve a "notice to owner" upon any person who appears to be the owner of the vehicle in question. If there is no response to that notice and the fixed penalty still remains unpaid, then a sum equal to the fixed penalty, plus one half of the amount of that penalty, may be registered for enforcement as a fine against the person to whom notice was sent. (s 32(2) TA 1982.)

(c) Procedure

The procedure for registration commences when the police issue a certificate known as a "fine registration certificate", which must be sent to the clerk to the justices for the petty sessions area in which the defaulter appears to reside (s 36(4) TA 1982).

The registration certificate must:

    (i)   give particulars of the offence to which the fixed penalty notice relates, namely:

- the serial number and date, time and place of issue of the notice to owner, notice to hirer or fixed penalty (as the case may be);
- the vehicle registration number;
- the driver number;
- the amount of the appropriate fixed penalty;
- the sum to be registered in default of payment of the fixed penalty;

    (ii)   indicate whether registration is authorised under s 30(3) or 32(2) of the 1982 Act; and
    (iii) state the name and last known address of the defaulter (s 36(5) TA 1982).

If the defaulter does not reside in that petty sessions area, then the clerk receiving the notice must cause the certificate to be forwarded on to the clerk to the justices for the petty sessions area (including Scotland) where the defendant does appear to reside (s 36(7) TA 1982). It should not be returned to the police force who issued the certificate or the fixed penalty clerk for that area.

On receipt of the registration certificate the clerk must register the sum for enforcement by entering it in the court register. Separate registers are kept for this purpose, although they are regarded as part of the main court register (s 36(6) TA 1982 and s 66(B) MCR 1981).

Notice is then required to be served on the defaulter at the address given in the certificate of registration, specifying the amount due and giving information about the offence and the authority for registration (s 36(8) TA 1982 and r 111 MCR 1981). In the case of limited companies, notice can be sent to either of the following addresses:

(i) the company's registered office; or
(ii) the address kept by the Driver and Vehicle Licensing Centre for the purpose of excise duty records.
(s 36(9) TA 1982).

See page 147 for the prescribed form of notice to defaulter.

If the certificate relates to an endorsable offence the clerk of any court receiving the registration certificate must also inform the fixed penalty clerk holding the relevant driving licence that the sum has been registered (Reg 8 Fixed Penalty (Procedure) Regulations 1986). See page 147 for the prescribed notice to the fixed penalty clerk.

Note that for these purposes a "person" includes a body both corporate and unincorporate and it would be wrong for any justices' clerk to refuse registration on the basis that an unincorporated association had no legal personality despite the obvious and practical difficulties of enforcement against that "person" (ss 31 and 36(1) TA 1982, Sch 1 Interpretation Act 1978).

(d) Effect of registration

On a fixed penalty being registered for enforcement it has effect as if the sum so registered were a fine imposed by that court on the conviction of the defaulter on the date of registration (s 36(10) and (11) TA 1982). Accordingly, the provisions of the MCA 1980 relating to the enforcement of fines apply and the power to remit fines contained in s 85 MCA 1980 is specifically included.

3. Challenging fine registration

(a) Statutory declarations

As stated earlier, it is inevitable that, with the many hundreds of thousands of tickets being issued, the system will occasionally falter and mistakes will occur. It is important therefore to appreciate that the Transport Act allows for the penalty to be challenged even after registration and before the full consequences of enforcement arise. Where the fixed penalty was registered by virtue of s 30(3) TA 1982 (driver present) the person who has received notice of the registration may invalidate it by making a statutory declaration to the effect that:

(i) he was not the person to whom the relevant fixed penalty notice was given; or

(ii) that he gave notice requesting a hearing in respect of the alleged offence as permitted by the fixed penalty notice *before* the end of the suspended enforcement period.

See page 148 for the prescribed form of statutory declaration (s 37(2) TA 1982).

Where the registration was made by virtue of s 32(2) TA 1982 (driver not present) the person who has received notice of the registration may invalidate it by making a statutory declaration to the effect that:

(i) he did not know of the fixed penalty notice concerned or of any fixed penalty notice or notice to owner relating to that penalty until he received notice of the registration; or

(ii) he was not the owner of the vehicle at the time of the alleged offence, and he has a reasonable excuse for failing to comply with the notice to owner; or

(iii) he gave notice requesting a hearing before the end of the period allowed under s 31 TA 1982 for response to the notice to owner

(s 37(3) TA 1982).

See page 149 for the prescribed form of statutory declaration.

The declaration must be made within twenty-one days of receiving notice of the registration, or of notice of any enforcement proceedings in respect of that registration, whichever is the earlier (s 37(1)(b) TA 1982). It must be served on the clerk of the court which registered the sum either by delivering it to him, leaving it at his office or by sending it by registered post or recorded delivery to his office (s 38(4) TA 1982). It is possible for a single justice to extend the time limit for making a statutory declaration in cases where the justice considers there to be reasonable grounds for delay (s 38(5) TA 1982).

(a) Effect of a statutory declaration

On receiving a statutory declaration the clerk should scrutinise it for error. If there is none, he must accept it and cancel the fine registration. If any error is found he should contact the declarant. It should always be pointed out to the declarant that any person who knowingly and wilfully makes a statutory declaration which is false in a material particular is guilty of an offence and liable on conviction to imprisonment or a fine, or both (s 5 Perjury Act 1911).

A copy of the statutory declaration must be sent to the appropriate chief officer of police immediately, so that he can consider what further action is necessary (r 112 MCR 1981).

Chapter 5

General provisions relating to the enforcement of maintenance orders

1. Introduction

"A maintenance order" means any order specified in Sch 8 Administration of Justice Act 1970. They are:

(a) an order for alimony, maintenance or other payments made, or having effect as if made, under Part II Matrimonial Causes Act 1973 (financial relief for parties to marriage and children of family);

(b) an order for payments to, or in respect of, a child, being an order made, or having effect as if made under Part III Matrimonial Causes Act 1973 (maintenance of children following divorce, etc);

(c) an order for periodical or other payments made, or having effect as if made, under Part II Matrimonial Causes Act 1973;

(d) an order for maintenance or other payments to, or in respect of a spouse or child, being an order made under Part I Domestic Proceedings and Magistrates' Courts Act 1978;

(e) an order under ss 11B, 11C or 11D Guardianship of Minors Act 1971, or s 2(3) or 2(4)(h) Guardianship Act 1973 (payments for maintenance of persons who are or have been in guardianship);

(f) an order under s 6 of the Family Law Reform Act 1969 (payments for maintenance of ward of court);

(g) an affiliation order, ie an order under s 4 Affiliation Proceedings Act 1957, s 44 National Assistance Act 1948, s 50 Child Care Act 1980, s 24 Ministry of Social Security Act 1966, s 45 Children Act 1975, s 19 Supplementary Benefits Act 1976, or s 25 Social Security Act

1986. Note that affiliation orders are repealed by Sch 2 para 27(b) Family Law Reform Act 1987 (when in force) but they are still maintenance orders for the purpose of payment and enforcement provided the order has not expired or arrears are outstanding

(h) an order under s 47 or 51 Child Care Act 1980; s 23 Ministry of Social Security Act 1966 or s 18 Supplementary Benefits Act 1976 (various provisions for obtaining contributions from a person whose dependants are assisted or maintained out of public funds);

(i) an order under s 43 National Assistance Act 1948 (recovery of costs of maintaining assisted person);

(j) an order to which s 16 Maintenance Orders Act 1950 applies by virtue of subs (2)(b) or (c) of that section, ie an order made by a court in Scotland or Northern Ireland and corresponding to one of those specified in the foregoing paragraphs) and which has been registered in a court in England and Wales under Part II of that Act;

(k) a maintenance order within the meaning of the Maintenance Orders (Facilities for Enforcement) Act 1920 (Commonwealth orders enforceable in the United Kingdom) registered in, or confirmed by, a court in England and Wales under that Act;

(l) an order for periodical or other payments made under Part II Matrimonial Proceedings and Property Act 1970;

(m) a maintenance order within the meaning of Part I Maintenance Orders (Reciprocal Enforcement) Act 1972 registered in a magistrates' court under the said Part I;

(n) a maintenance order within the meaning of Part I Civil Jurisdiction and Judgments Act 1982 which is registered in a magistrates' court under that Part;

(o) an order under s 34(1)(b) Children Act 1975 (payments of maintenance in respect of a child to his custodian);

(p) an order for periodical or other payments made under Part III of the Matrimonial and Family Proceedings Act 1984.

All the above orders are either "maintenance orders" able to be made by a magistrates' court or are orders "enforceable as a magistrates' court maintenance order" in the magistrates' court.

MCA 1980 and the MCR 1981 prescribe most of the procedures

General provisions relating to the enforcement of maintenance orders

for the enforcement of such orders, but before dealing with these it is worth discussing other factors which may affect the enforcement of a maintenance order.

2. Factors which may affect the enforcement of a maintenance order

(a) Bankruptcy

Maintenance arrears are not recoverable in bankruptcy as the value of the debt is "incapable of being fairly estimated" within the requirements of bankruptcy law. Nevertheless, proceedings may still be taken for enforcement against a person who is bankrupt or subject to bankruptcy proceedings *(James* v *James* (1963)).

(b) Death

If either the person liable to make payments, or the person entitled to receive payment, dies, the general position is that the order, together with the power to enforce, will cease.

Arrears owing to a party at the time of that party's death cannot be recovered in a magistrates' court by that party's legal representative, but any moneys in the possession of the court collecting officer at the time of death are part of the deceased's estate *(Re Green (A Bankrupt), ex parte Official Receiver* v *Cutting* (1979)). Arrears owed by a defendant who dies cannot be recovered against his estate *(Re Bidie, Bidie* v *General Accident Fire and Life Assurance Corporation Ltd* (1948)). No authority exists about the effect of death upon an order expressed to be paid direct to a child (as opposed to the mother for the benefit of the child), or an order expressed to be paid through a third party. It is submitted, however, that death of the complainant does not terminate an order under which money is paid direct to a child because of the personal nature of the order between the payer and the child. Similarly, it is submitted that an order for payment through a third party will not lapse upon the death of the original complainant. See also 151 JPN 160.

(c) Dissolution of marriage and remarriage

A marriage which has been dissolved since the making of the maintenance order does not prevent the order from being enforced *(Wood* v *Wood* (1957)). Likewise an order may be enforced even though the party to whom the arrears are due has remarried.

(d) Discharge

Where an order has been discharged it remains a maintenance order for the purpose of enforcement provided there are still arrears to be recovered (s 150 MCA 1980).

(e) Repealed legislation

A maintenance order made under legislation which has since been repealed (eg the Matrimonial Proceedings (Magistrates' Courts) Act 1960) remains a maintenance order for the purposes of payment and enforcement provided the order has not expired and/ or arrears are outstanding.

(f) Appeal

There is nothing to prevent an order being enforced pending an appeal, though generally it would be quite wrong to do so. In *Kendal* v *Wilkinson* (1855) Lord Campbell CJ said:

> "In the vast majority of cases it would be exceedingly improper for a justice to grant a warrant after the notice . . . and before the hearing of the appeal . . ., but I do not think that in granting it he could be said to have acted without jurisdiction."

Lord Campbell remarked on the inequity that would arise where the defendant, never intending to prosecute the appeal, could "as a matter of right entirely escape all liability to contribute".

Kendall v *Wilkinson* establishes the principle (confirmed in *R* v *Wilmot* (1861)) that, while it is lawful to enforce the order pending an appeal against it, it would be improper where the appeal is *bona fide*. This is difficult to reconcile with *R* v *Durham Justices* (1891) in which it was held that the court to which the appeal was being made is the exclusive judge of the sufficiency of the grounds. Quite clearly, there would have to be exceptional circumstances before the order was enforced. However, that does not mean that the clerk is entitled to withhold money from the other party pending an appeal. In *Board* v *Board* (1981) Holin J said "that the bringing of an appeal did not operate as a stay on the proceedings", and the clerk was wrong in withholding money from the wife.

(g) Validity

Where there has been no appeal or where an appeal has been unsuccessful, the court may not concern itself with the validity of the order to be enforced *(Sammy-Joe* v *GPO Mount Pleasant Office and Another* (1966)).

General provisions relating to the enforcement of maintenance orders

(h) Imprisonment

Imprisonment or other detention for failing to pay maintenance arrears does not discharge the defendant from his liability to pay. He cannot, however, be imprisoned or detained a second time in respect of the same arrears (s 93(8) MCA 1980 and s 17 Maintenance Order Act 1958).

(i) Registration

An order registered in a magistrates' court (see Chapter 7) is enforceable in that court and cannot be enforced, during the subsistence of registration, in the court which originally made it. This does not mean that enforcement proceedings can be taken only in the court of registration. It is neither the purpose of the Maintenance Order Act 1950 ("MOA 1950") nor of the Maintenance Order Act 1958 ("MOA 1958") to limit the hearing of enforcement proceedings to a single magistrates' court. The more fundamental purpose is to give magistrates' courts in England and Wales jurisdiction to entertain proceedings in relation to orders which they could not themselves have made. Registered orders can be enforced in all respects as if they had been made by the court of registration, and consequently r 59 Magistrates' Courts Rules 1987 will apply, allowing proceedings to be heard elsewhere than in the court of registration (s 18(6) MOA 1950 and s 3(4) MOA 1958). For the registration of maintenance orders generally see Chapter 7.

(j) Further proceedings

Proceedings can be taken to enforce payment of a sum due and unpaid under a maintenance order notwithstanding that a previous complaint has been made in respect of that sum, or a part thereof, and whether or not an order was made in those previous proceedings (s 20(8) MOA 1958).

3. Procedures for enforcement

(a) The court collecting officer

Until 1914, the responsibility for enforcing a maintenance order lay with the claimant. The Affiliation Orders Act 1914 gave justices a discretion to direct that maintenance payments be made through a third party (usually the justices' clerk), thus abolishing the necessity for the claimant to have any further communication with the payer. In 1935 these arrangements were revised and extended. The present position is that a "justices' clerk is, by virtue of his office, collecting officer of any magistrates' court of which he is clerk". However, the clerk is not the agent of the justices when he receives payments in his capacity as court collecting officer *(O'Connor* v *Isaacs* (1956)).

As collecting officer, a justices' clerk has a duty to discharge all functions that are conferred on him by enactments relating to the collection, payment and enforcement of maintenance.

(b) Notification of arrears

Where an order requires periodical payments to be made to the clerk of a magistrates' court and the payments are at any time in arrears to an amount equal to four times the weekly sum (or, in the case of payments to be made monthly or less frequently, twice the sum payable periodically), the clerk must give written particulars of the arrears to the person entitled to receive them, unless it appears to the clerk unnecessary or inexpedient to do so (r 40 MCR 1981). While the rules provide for notice to be given only once, in practice most courts will do this on a more regular basis, and indeed many accounting systems, particularly computerised, provide a continuous update of information.

Previous rules provided that special circumstances were required before the clerk could exercise his discretion not to give notice. Accordingly, it used to be said that regular appearances at the clerk's office by the person to whom notice was to be given were not special as in fact they were an everyday occurrence. The rules no longer require special circumstances and it is therefore submitted that it would be unnecessary to give notice where a person regularly calls at the clerk's office and is kept fully informed of the arrears position.

No form of notice is prescribed by the rules.

(c) Net or gross arrears

Where the order to be enforced is a gross order, (ie not a small maintenance order), then responsibility for the payment of income tax at the basic rate falls on the payer. It would, however, be wrong to argue that only the net amount should appear on any complaint, summons or warrant, for unless a certificate of deduction is given to the justices' clerk and credit is given (which can arise only when payment is made), the gross amount remains due, and the account and any enforcement action should show the gross amount. It would, of course, be possible for a payer who is

General provisions relating to the enforcement of maintenance orders

about to be arrested on warrant, to pay the arresting officer the net amount together with the appropriate tax forms but we suspect the subtlety of this transaction would be lost on the officer concerned!

(d) The complaint

Proceedings are begun by complaint. Where periodical payments are being made by one person to another person under more than one order, then proceedings for enforcement may be brought using only one complaint, provided the complaint indicates the payments that are due under each order (s 93(1) MCA 1980). In establishing the amount of arrears due under each order (excluding lump sums), the provisions contained in r 60(2) MCR 1981 relating to apportionment should be considered.

No form of complaint is now prescribed; the Affiliation Proceedings Act 1957, which preserved the Bastardy (Forms) Order 1915, was repealed by the Family Law Reform Act 1987.

Under the Justices' Clerks Rules 1970 the complaint can be made to either a justice of the peace or, if not, on oath, to a justices' clerk, by

(i) the person entitled to payments, including, in the case of a child, the person with whom the child has his home (s 62(1) MCA 1980); or

(ii) the clerk to the justices (where the order requires payments through the court) if required to do so in writing by the person entitled to payments (s 59(3) MCA (1980).

In the latter case, the clerk must take proceedings unless it appears to him to be unreasonable in the circumstances to do so (s 59(4) MCA 1980). A refusal by the clerk to act in his own name will not prevent the person entitled to payments from taking proceedings on his own account. In practice, however, the first action will usually come from the clerk who will request from the person entitled to payment an "authority to enforce". Surprisingly, this is not always forthcoming. If the clerk does take proceedings in his own name the liability for costs properly incurred in the proceedings falls on the person requesting the clerk as if he had made the complaint himself.

(e) Jurisdiction

Rule 59(1) MCR 1981 provides that a complaint for the enforcement of an affiliation order, or an order enforceable as an affiliation order, must be heard by the court that made the order. There are two exceptions to this rule. Where:

(i)
- the complainant is the person in whose favour the order was made, and
- the complainant resides in a petty sessions area other than that for which the court acts, and
- payment is directed to be made either to the complainant or the clerk of a magistrates' court acting for that petty sessions area,

the complaint can then be heard by the last-mentioned court;

(ii) where the complainant is the clerk of a magistrates' court, the complaint may be heard by that court.

These exceptions, however, do not apply to the enforcement of a child care contribution order which is to be heard only by the court having jurisdiction in the place where the person liable to pay is residing (r 59(7) MCR 1981 and s 47(4) Child Care Act 1980).

(f) Transfer of proceedings

Where a complaint is made to a justice of the peace for the enforcement of a magistrates' court maintenance order (including a registered order) and it appears to him that the defendant is for the time being in some other petty sessions area and that the order may be more conveniently enforced by a magistrates' court acting for that area, the justice shall cause the clerk of the court ("the administering court") to send the complaint by post to the clerk for that other area (r 59(2) MCR 1981). The Home Office has suggested that any information likely to assist the other court in its proceedings should also accompany the complaint. A complaint not on oath may be made to a justices' clerk who may also make a determination as to venue.

On receipt of the complaint the other court must either issue a summons, or if the complaint purports to be on oath, a warrant, for procuring the appearance of the defendant before it. It may then hear and determine the complaint (r 59(3) MCR 1981).

If money is received under the order after the complaint has been sent to the other court, the clerk of the court receiving payment must immediately send a certificate stating the date and the amount of the payment. Similarly, if any payments are made direct to the person entitled to receive payments, that person must forthwith inform the clerk to whom the complaint was originally made in order that he may inform the clerk of the court

General provisions relating to the enforcement of maintenance orders

subsequently dealing with the matter. Rule 59(6) MCR 1981 provides that any certificate issued under this procedure and signed by the clerk of the court to whom the complaint was originally made is admissible as evidence of the amount specified and date of payment specified. It is submitted, however, that unless there is strong evidence to the contrary, the other court should always treat any certified payment as having been appropriated to the arrears and nothing else. No form of certificate of payment is prescribed by the rules.

In deciding whether to transfer proceedings, it need only appear to the administering court that the defendant "is for the time being" in some other area, and not that the defendant resides there. Furthermore, as it is the administering court which determines that the order may be more conveniently enforced by another magistrates' court, there appears to be no way in which the other court can refuse to act.

In practice, however, if the administering court becomes aware that the defendant is in yet another court area, or even back within its own jurisdiction, it will seek to withdraw proceedings from the transferred venue and start again. Similarly, if attempts by the other court to trace the defendant are unsuccessful the other court will usually return the complaint giving the original court such information as it has managed to ascertain about the whereabouts of the defendant.

Where any decision is reached, or warrant of distress or commitment is issued, in pursuance of a complaint relating to the enforcement of a maintenance order, being a complaint heard by a court other than the administering court, then the clerk of that court must immediately send to the clerk of the administering court an extract from the court register containing the decision. On receipt of that extract the clerk of the administering court must enter the particulars in his court register (r 21 Magistrates' Courts (Maintenance Orders Act 1958) Rules 1959) See page 150 for the prescribed form of extract.

(g) Summons and warrant

Once a complaint has been laid, invariably a summons will be issued directing the defaulter to appear before the court. However, if the complaint has been substantiated on oath, a warrant without bail may be issued for the defendant's arrest whether or not a summons has previously been issued (s 93(5) MCA 1980). Despite this, a court should only issue a warrant in the first instance if satisfied that a summons would be ineffective. No form of summons or warrant is prescribed.

(h) Time limits

Proceedings cannot be commenced earlier than the fifteenth day after the making of the order (s 93(2) MCA 1980). Unlike civil debt, it is not necessary to serve a copy of the order on the defendant before it can be enforced. In practice, however, a copy of the order will have been served before proceedings began. From the fifteenth day after the making of the order onwards a complaint can be made at any time.

(i) Payment and discharge of process

It is the practice of all courts to dispense with the defaulter's attendance if the amount due is paid, in full, before the return date. This practice derives from the wording of Form 18 of the Bastardy (Forms) Order 1915, as amended by the Bastardy (Forms) Order 1935, previously the appropriate form of warrant. The relevant words, "unless the said sum and all costs and charges be sooner paid", were in brackets and could be deleted if the justices thought fit. If the words were struck out the constable executing the warrant had no power to receive the amount due and had to bring the defaulter to court as directed by the warrant. In the case of a persistent defaulter who could afford to pay but was prepared to put the complainant, the court and the police to constant trouble, this was a useful way of ensuring that he could be told of the trouble he caused. The repeal of the Bastardy (Form) Order 1935 leaves the continuance of this practice in some doubt.

(j) Tracing missing defendants

No amount of legislation will produce any money if the defendant cannot be found. As a last resort, certain government departments are prepared to assist in tracing missing defendants if information such as a National Insurance number or a photograph is supplied to them. If they are able to assist, any information is supplied on the strict understanding that it will be used only for the purpose of the proceedings and not supplied to anyone else. The procedure to be used is described in detail in Home Office Circular 140/1971 and Practice Direction [1973] 1 All ER 61. The addresses to which enquiries about former servicemen are to be sent are contained in Practice Direction [1979] 2 All ER 1106.

4. The hearing

(a) Domestic proceedings

Enforcement proceedings are not automatically domestic proceedings, but certain provisions applicable to domestic proceedings, such as the power to require a report on the means of the parties, and the duty to assist an unrepresented party who is unable to examine or cross-examine a witness effectively, apply also to enforcement (ss 72 and 73 MCA 1980). The justices may, if they think fit, order that the proceedings be treated as domestic proceedings, in which case other provisions, such as reporting restrictions, can be applied (s 65(2) MCA 1980). This practice is strongly recommended, as justices who are not domestic panel members are often ill-equipped to cope with the complexities of maintenance enforcement.

(b) Proof of non-payment

Proof of non-payment may take either of the following forms, unless the court requires the clerk or other person to be called as a witness:

(i) if the person to whom the sum is ordered to be paid is a clerk of a magistrates' court, a certificate purporting to be signed by the clerk that the sum has not been paid to him; and

(ii) in any other case a document purporting to be a statutory declaration by the person to whom the sum was ordered to be paid that the sum has not been paid to him

(s 99 MCA 1980).

The certificate or declaration can, of course, be rebutted. See pages 150 and 151 for the prescribed forms.

(c) Means inquiry reports

In proceedings for the enforcement of a maintenance order made in "domestic proceedings" as defined in s 65(1) MCA 1980, the court can direct a probation officer to investigate the means of the parties, and require him to provide the court with either a written report of his investigations or an oral statement (s 72 MCA 1980).

Where the court requires a written report, a copy must be given to each party to the proceedings or their legal representative. The court may, if it thinks fit, require the report (or such part of it as it specifies) to be read aloud at the hearing.

The court or either of the parties to the proceedings can require that the probation officer attend to give evidence about his investigations. Either party may give or call evidence with respect to any matter contained in the report or in the evidence given by the officer.

Both the report and the evidence of the officer can be received by the court, notwithstanding any provision that would otherwise make these matters inadmissible as evidence. This exception is indeed sensible, as most investigative reports rely heavily on hearsay and the court would otherwise be deprived of relevant and useful information. However, great care must be taken to distinguish statement of fact from statement of opinion.

(d) Adjournments

Proceedings for enforcement can be adjourned, but the defendant cannot be remanded (s 93(3) and (4) MCA 1980). The court can proceed in his absence if it is proved to the satisfaction of the court that the summons was served within what appears to be a reasonable time before the hearing, or that the defendant has previously appeared (r 67 MCR 1981). Appearances may be made by solicitor or counsel except, for example, where personal appearance is required by recognizance (s 122 MCA 1980).

(e) Remission of arrears

On the hearing of a complaint for the enforcement of a magistrates' court maintenance order, the court can remit the whole or any part of the sum due under the order (s 95 MCA 1980). However, before doing so, the court must, unless it appears unnecessary or impracticable to do so, notify the person in whose favour the order was made and allow that person a reasonable opportunity to make representations to the court, either orally or in writing (r 44 MCR 1981). Any written representations may be considered by the court if they are purportedly signed by or on behalf of the person entitled to payments. No form of notice is prescribed by the rules. *Certiorari* will follow if r 44 is not complied with (*R v Dover Magistrates' Court, ex parte Kidner* (1983)).

No guidance is given as to when it would be "unnecessary" or "impracticable" to give notice. Presumably where the court already has an agreement to the remission from the person entitled to payments then notice would be unnecessary. Other examples might include a long history of non-response by the person entitled to payment, or where the whereabouts of that person are no longer known. It is suggested, however, that any doubt should be resolved in favour of the person entitled to payment and the matter adjourned for notice to be given.

General provisions relating to the enforcement of maintenance orders

The rules are very clear as to whom notice is to be given. This does not include the DHSS, unless the order has been made in their favour.

The rules do not specify a specific form of notice, merely what the notice should contain. Experience has shown, however, that many people are not familiar with the word "remit" and, where possible, a simple form of explanation should be used.

"It will be a matter entirely for the magistrate's discretion on the light of the evidence before him whether to enforce or to remit as he thinks proper the whole or any part of the sum due . . ." per Lord Meriman P, *Pilcher* v *Pilcher* (No 2) (1956). In exercising their discretion to remit, it has been said that justices should usually follow the practice of the Family Division and enforce only arrears which have accrued within the year before the date of complaint. This is only a rule of practice, although it is usually followed. The court can consider whether, in the circumstances of any given case, it is right to follow the practice either in whole or in part. The practice was approved and followed in *Luscombe* v *Luscombe* (1962) and *Freeman-Thomas* v *Freeman-Thomas* (1963). In *Ross* v *Pearson* (1976) it was established that while the practice could be appropriately used in the magistrates' court, there was an absolute rule preventing the enforcement of arrears more than one year old. Thus, in *Russell* v *Russell* (1985) it was held that the fact that a consent order had been made in the county court within twelve months of the complaint was a justifiable reason for distinguising the case from the usual case where "stale arrears" were being considered. However, it was held in *Dickens* v *Pattison* (1985) that the mere fact that the person liable to pay the maintenance was an irregular or reluctant payer was not an unusual circumstance, and did not justify departure from the normal rule. Sir John Donaldson MC in *Russell* v *Russell* said that justices who consider they have a "discretion to remit" are misdirecting themselves; the "discretion" is one to "enforce".

Whilst the court has power to remit any sum due and unpaid at the date of the complaint, it has no power to remit any sums already paid to the collecting officer and held by him (*Fildes (formerly Simkin)* v *Simkin* (1959)).

The power to remit is clearly an exercise of the court's discretion, which like all discretions, must be exercised judicially and not capriciously. Therefore, remission of arrears due to a wife is not justified simply because she has impeded the defendant's right to have access to his children. Since maintenance payments are not a reward for allowing access, remission should not be imposed as a penalty for refusing it; see *R* v *Halifax Justices, ex parte Woolverton* (1978).

It is an improper use of the justices' discretion to remit arrears to satisfy payment of a mother's debt where the maintenance payments are payable to the child and belong to the child *(Parry* v *Meugens* (1985)).

In *R* v *Blackpool Justices, ex parte Ardullis* (1981) Sir John Arnold, President of the Family Division, sitting as an additional Judge of the Queen's Bench Division, said that it was open to the court to quash a decision of the justices to remit arrears of maintenance. In *R* v *Dover Magistrates' Court, ex parte Kidner* (1983) an order for *certiorari* was granted and the decision to remit the arrears was quashed on the court's failure to comply with r 44 MCR 1981.

(f) Power to search

The court can direct that the defendant be searched and may apply any money found in his possession in satisfaction of the arrears, unless the defendant can satisfy the court that the money does not belong to him or that the loss of the money would be more injurious to his family than would be his detention (s 80 MCA 1980).

(g) Arrears arising since complaint made

Fresh arrears which have become due since the complaint was made should be dealt with by the same court. An application to amend the complaint must be made, or a new complaint made and the old one withdrawn.

(h) Notice of decision

The court must give notice in writing to the complainant of its decision on a complaint for the enforcement of a maintenance order, unless the complainant is present or is the clerk of the court (r 61 MCR 1981). No form of notice is prescribed by the rules.

(i) Costs

The court has a discretion to order such costs as it thinks just and reasonable, and, whatever adjudication it makes, the court can order either side to pay the whole or part of the other side's costs (s 64(1) and (4) MCA 1980). Costs ordered against the defendant can be enforced with the maintenance arrears.

General provisions relating to the enforcement of maintenance orders

5. Appeal

(a) Appeal by way of case stated

No appeal to the Crown Court is provided for, but appeal, by way of case stated, lies to the Family Division of the High Court (s 111 MCA 1980 and RSC O 56 r 5(2)(a)). However, in *Snape* v *Snape* (1983) the Family Division felt able to consider the question of arrears on the substantive appeal. Yet in *Mills* v *Mills* (1982) the Family Division, in very similar circumstances, declined to treat the justices' refusal to remit arrears as part of the appeal on *quantum* of maintenance. In *Allen* v *Allen* (1985) Mrs Justice Booth was not so reticent. Her Ladyship held that the refusal of the justices to remit the arrears was part of their refusal to vary the order itself. Both the orders were made upon an application to vary and therefore the right of appeal to the High Court by way of notice of motion extended to the refusal to remit the arrears. A contrary view, however, was taken by Sir John Arnold in *Fletcher* v *Fletcher* (1985). He stated that the remission of arrears under an application to vary was an intrinsic part of the enforcement procedure from which appeal was by way of case stated only. This was followed in *Berry* v *Berry* (1986) and appears to settle the matter beyond doubt.

In *R* v *Horseferry Road Magistrates' Court, ex parte Bernstein* (1987) the question arose whether a magistrate could refuse to state a case on the ground that his decision was not final, since before the order of commitment to prison could be issued, the court was required to review the matter under s 18 MOA 1958. Sir John Arnold held that although a magistrates' court had power to review a committal order, the decision, even though on suspended terms, was a final one and suitable for argument on a case stated (*Streames* v *Copping* (1985) distinguished).

(b) Appeal by way of judicial review

Application may be made in appropriate cases for judicial review. In *R* v *Dover Magistrates' Court, ex parte Kidner* (1983) Mr Justice Woolf stated that when judicial review is sought in respect of a matrimonial or family order, the application should include a request that it be heard by a Family Division judge rather than by a Queen's Bench Division judge. Proceedings by way of judicial review in relation to enforcement proceedings are in no way different to those in relation to orders or convictions in general, and are governed by RSC O 53.

6. Maintenance orders made against members of Her Majesty's forces

(a) Deductions from pay made by the service authorities

The usual method of enforcing an order for the maintenance of dependants made against a person who is, or becomes, a member of Her Majesty's Forces is by means of deductions from his pay by the service authorities. This is in accordance with the provisions of s 150 of the Army and Air Force Acts 1955, as amended by the Army and Air Force Act 1961, and s 1 Naval Forces (Enforcement of Maintenance Liabilities) Act 1947. See also Home Office Circular 251/1970. The sums, payment of which may be enforced by this means, are sums due in respect of the maintenance of:

(i) a man's wife or child; or
(ii) any illegitimate child of whom he is the putative father; or
(iii) in the case of a soldier or airman, any child, legitimate or illegitimate, of his wife.

An order requiring a member of the Royal Navy or Royal Marines to make maintenance payments in respect of a child who is not his child is not enforceable by deductions from his pay by the naval authorities. In such a case it would be helpful to the naval authorities if the justices' clerk, on sending the order to the Director General of Defence Accounts, would draw attention to the fact that one or more of the children named in the order is not the child of the man against whom the order is made.

(b) Alternative to deductions from pay

There are, however, signs that the service authorities are finding the compulsory deduction of pay, regardless of willingness to pay, time-consuming and expensive; see Home Office Circular 25/1986. Consequently, the Ministry of Defence changed the procedures for the deduction of maintenance payments in respect of army personnel from 1 September 1985. The individual is now encouraged to make his own arrangements to meet his obligations under the court order. Should the serviceman disregard the court order or default at any time, application may then be made to the service authorities for enforcement of the order under s 150 Army Act 1955 and the Minimum Rates of Pay (Army) Order 1982.

(c) Collection of arrears

A change has also taken place concerning the collection of arrears.

General provisions relating to the enforcement of maintenance orders

In the past, army regimental paymasters kept a record of all arrears accruing, and recovered these arrears in instalments once the serviceman was in a position to pay. Under the revised procedure arrears will not be recovered automatically; the authorities suggest that it will be necessary for the complainant to obtain a further court order which, if made as a lump sum, can be enforced against pay under s 151A Army Act 1955. Precisely what sort of further order can be obtained in the magistrates' court remains a mystery, for in law the maintenance order and the arrears are indivisible. Furthermore, s 151A Army Act 1955 caters for the enforcement of civil debt, the definition of which, in the magistrates' court, specifically excludes maintenance payments. It should be emphasised, however, that these changes affect army personnel only.

(d) Transmission of an order to the service authorities

A court making an order which is to be enforced by the service authorities by means of deductions from pay is required to send a copy of the order to the appropriate service authority as follows:

The Army

All ranks except officers:	The Regimental Paymaster (see the list of addresses in Appendix C to the Home Office Circular 61/1972)
Officers:	Ministry of Defence PS4d (Army), Room 1001, Empress State Building, London SW6 1TR

The Royal Air Force

All ranks except officers:	The Director of Personnel Management, (ADP) (RAF), Ministry of Defence, RAF Personnel Management Centre PM(ADP) 22c (RAF), Innsworth Gloucester GL3 1E2
Officers:	The Under-Secretary of State for Defence for the Royal Air Force, P6a (RAF), Room 308, Adastral House Theobalds Road London WC1X 8RU

The Royal Navy and Royal Marines All ranks:	Director General of Defence Accounts, HMS Centurion, Pay & Pensions Division Branch PP3C(ii), Grange Road Gosport, Hants PO13 9XA

The arrangements described above apply to maintenance orders against members of Her Majesty's Forces whether the order is made before or after the man's enlistment.

(e) Enforcement after cessation of service

In the case of former army and air force personnel the full range of enforcement powers, including committal, is available whether the arrears accrued before, during, or after his service (s 1(3) Naval Forces (Enforcement of Maintenance Liabilities) Act 1947). However, as regards the Royal Navy and Royal Marines no committal may be ordered in respect of arrears accrued during the service of any seaman or marine unless the court is satisfied that he is able or has, since he ceased to serve, been able to pay the arrears, and has failed to do so.

(f) Distress

A member of the armed forces is not immune from the execution of a distress warrant for the enforcement of a maintenance order, save as to the arms, ammunition, equipment, instruments or clothing used by him for naval, military or air force purposes (s 185 Army and Air Force Acts 1955, and s 102 Naval Discipline Act 1957). In practice, however, it would be highly unlikely that any bailiff would be allowed access to Ministry of Defence property in order to execute the warrant in respect of the defendant's personal property.

(g) Reserve and Auxiliary Forces

The protection afforded by the Reserve and Auxiliary Forces (Protection of Civil Interests) Act 1951 does not extend to arrears under a maintenance order.

7. Visiting forces

The enforcement of an order made against a member of a visiting armed force will very much depend on whether that person is still within the jurisdiction. If so, then his position is no different from

General provisions relating to the enforcement of maintenance orders

that of any other civilian, save that the Home Office has asked to be informed before any warrant of commitment is issued (Home Office Circular 122/1954). It is assumed that the diplomatic channels will be used to try to produce an amicable settlement. If the person has left the jurisdiction, enforcement will be reciprocal, subject to such arrangements existing.

Chapter 6

Imprisonment for non-payment of maintenance

1. Introduction

Imprisonment is a sanction both harsh and severe in its consequences to the defendant and expensive to the state. In its effect upon a man's character, his family and dependants, the interruption of his work and the possibility of not finding work upon his release, it is often out of all proportion to the default of which he has been guilty. It is therefore essential that it should never be imposed without careful consideration, and should only be resorted to if it is the only practicable way of enforcing compliance with the law or with obligations which in the public interest must be enforced. It is particularly important that the sanction should not be used mechanically or automatically. The law does not require justices to commit where it is clearly undesirable to do so; see *Grocock* v *Grocock* (1920).

2. Restrictions on the use of imprisonment

(a) Inquiry into cause of default

A magistrates' court cannot impose imprisonment for a default to which a complaint relates unless it has inquired, in the presence of the defendant, whether the default was caused by the defendant's wilful refusal or culpable neglect; and it must not impose imprisonment if it is of the opinion that the default was not so due (s 93(6) MCA 1980). The onus of showing to the satisfaction of the justices that the default was not due to wilful refusal or culpable neglect is placed on the defendant (*James* v *James* (1963), per Sir Jocelyn Simon P).

(b) Necessity to consider attachment of earnings order

A magistrates' court cannot impose imprisonment in a case in which it has power to make an attachment of earnings order unless it is of the opinion that such an order would be inappropriate. Quite clearly, where the circumstances of the case are such that the defendant would frustrate the order of the court by changing his employment frequently, an attachment of earnings order would not be appropriate (s 93(6)(a) MCA 1980).

(c) Presence of defendant a prerequisite

A magistrates' court cannot impose imprisonment in the absence of the defendant (s 93(6)(b) MCA 1980). His presence at any previous hearing would not suffice.

3. Restrictions on the detention of young persons

It is not possible to commit a person under seventeen years to any form of custody for default (s 9 CJA 1982).

Where a court would, but for the general restriction on custodial sentences in relation to persons aged seventeen to twenty have power:

- (a) to commit a young person to prison for default in payment of any sum of money, or
- (b) to make a postponed committal order in the event of such default,

then the court may commit that young person to be detained, or may fix a term of detention in the event of default.

Any person dealt with in this way will be detained in one of the following places:

- (a) a remand centre;
- (b) a detention centre (young offenders institution under CJA 1988);
- (c) a youth custody centre (young offenders institution under CJA 1988); or
- (d) in any place in which a person aged 21 years or over could be kept for default in payment of a sum of money as the Secretary of State may from time to time direct (s 12(10) CJA 1982).

The power to detain is subject to the proviso that the court must be of the opinion that no other method of dealing with the offender is appropriate (s 1(5) CJA 1982). The reasons for reaching this opinion must be stated in open court and specified in the warrant and court register (s 2(5) and (7) CJA 1982).

4. The term of imprisonment

The period for which a defendant may be committed to prison under a warrant of commitment must not exceed six weeks (s 93(7) MCA 1980). The periods contained in Sch 4 MCA 1980 (see page 27 and note these periods will be reduced under CJA 1988) apply, as does the minimum period of five days. For example, maintenance arrears over £100 and under £400 would not carry imprisonment in excess of 30 days, and arrears exceeding £400 would be limited to a maximum of 42 days. See Home Office Circular 31/1979. See page 151 for the prescribed form of warrant (page 152 for the appropriate form where issue has been postponed).

A warrant of commitment, once issued, does not discharge the defendant from liability to pay the amount for which he was committed, although he cannot be committed again in respect of that amount or any part of it (s 93(8) MCA 1980 and s 17 MOA 1958). The one exception would be where the court cancelled the warrant of commitment on review before the expiry of the term and placed the defendant on a suspended warrant of commitment for the amount remaining due.

Despite the fact that a warrant of commitment does not discharge the defendant, in practice collecting officers mark these arrears as unenforceable. It is submitted, however, that nothing will prevent the court from making an attachment of earnings order in respect of the arrears for which imprisonment has been served, since the prohibition only forbids re-committal, and does not affect any other method of enforcement.

In the unlikely event that a person is made the subject of two postponed committals to prison for non-payment of two separate maintenance orders, it is possible to order that the terms of imprisonment run consecutively up to a maximum period of twelve weeks. However, this may be done only when the terms are originally fixed, not on review under s 18 of the Maintenance Orders Act 1958 (see page 72), since at that stage the court is not "imposing imprisonment" but simply issuing a warrant of imprisonment already imposed (note that "imposing imprisonment" includes fixing a term of imprisonment for failure to pay any sum of money).

5. Effect of committal on arrears

Unless the court directs otherwise (and very few will) no arrears will accrue while the defendant is in custody (s 94 MCA 1980). After release, the defendant may appropriate payments made to any new debt arising. In practice, however, few defendants take advantage of this and payments are appropriated against the earliest debt, ie the unenforceable debt for which imprisonment has alrady been served. Therefore, as the unenforceable arrears are discharged, further arrears accrue which *are* enforceable by imprisonment. A direction that arrears will accrue while he is in custody may properly be made where the defendant is deliberately avoiding the order *(Starkey* v *Starkey* (1954)).

6. Postponing a warrant of commitment

Where a magistrates' court has power to issue a warrant of commitment, it may, if it thinks fit to do so, fix a term of imprisonment and postpone the issue of the warrant until such time and on such conditions, if any, as it thinks just (s 77(2) MCA 1980).

In practice a term of imprisonment will be suspended in this way either upon payment of a single periodical amount (sufficient to cover current dues and something towards the arrears); or, preferably, on payment of the current order and a further amount towards the arrears. It is inappropriate for a committal order to be suspended for payment only of an additional amount in relation to the arrears (*Fowler* v *Fowler* (1981)).

Failure to fulfil any conditions attached to the postponement may result in the warrant being issued after review, but arrears that have accrued since the original grant of the warrant cannot be added on; and further proceedings will be necessary to secure committal in respect of those new arrears *(R* v *Governor of Bedford Prison, ex parte Ames* (1953)).

If the issue of the warrant of commitment is postponed on condition that the defendant pay the order together with further payments to cover arrears to which the order does not apply, all amounts paid thereafter should first be appropriated to the arrears in respect of which the committal order was made. This does not depend on the law relating to appropriation of payments, but solely on the statutory provisions relating to the power to commit, and the husband's right to avoid committal by paying the arrears *(R* v *Miskin Lower Justices, ex parte Young* (1953); *Johnson* v *Johnson* (1946)). In this way the committal order remains throughout the sanction for the non-payment of the original debt only (ie the specific sum mentioned in the complaint and proved to the justices to be in arrears).

Finally, there is nothing to prevent justices imposing any other conditions they think just, subject of course to their being reasonable and relevant.

7. Power to review committals

(a) Application not to have warrant of commitment issued

Where a warrant of commitment has been postponed, it must not subsequently be issued without further consideration (s 18(1) MOA 1958). The clerk to the justices is required to give notice to the person liable to make payments under the order that if he considers there are grounds for not issuing the warrant, he may apply to the court in the prescribed manner, requesting that the warrant should not be issued, and stating his grounds.

When dealing with orders not payable through his court, it is incumbent on the clerk to be extremely vigilant before acting on any notice of arrears supplied to him by the person entitled to receive payments.

Rule 22(1) Magistrates' Courts (Maintenance Orders Act 1958) Rules 1959 ("MC (MOA 1958) R 1959") prescribes the form of notice to be used by the clerk, as well as providing for a prescribed form of application which is to be attached to the notice. Such notice is deemed to be given to the defendant if it is sent by registered post or recorded delivery to his last known address (s 18(8) MOA 1958); notice is still deemed to have been given even if the notice is returned undelivered, or the defendant is known to have left that address *(Re Follick, ex parte Trustee* (1907)). See pages 153 and 154 for the prescribed forms of notice and application.

If, within eight days beginning with the day on which the clerk sends the notice to the defendant, the court has not received an application, then any justice of the peace acting for the same petty sessions area may issue the warrant of commitment (r 22(3) MC (MOA 1958)R 1959). This seems to indicate that the justice has a discretion in the matter, but it is hard to envisage many circumstances where the exercise of a discretion not to issue the warrant would be proper, and one would normally expect the warrant to be issued fairly promptly.

If, however, an application is received within the eight days, then any justice, as above, may, after considering its contents:

    (i) if of the opinion that the application should be further considered, refer it to the court; or

Imprisonment for non-payment of maintenance

    (ii)   if not of that opinion, issue the warrant forthwith.

Once again the justice involved has a limited discretion in the matter, although it has been said that he should always refer the matter to the court if there is a *prima facie* change in the defendant's circumstances *(Wood* v *Warley Justices* (1974)). Communications to a defendant at this stage, which could be interpreted as a modification of the notice given by the court of its intention to issue a warrant, should be sent by recorded delivery *(Slater* v *Calder Justices* (1984)).

If the application is to be referred to the court then s 18(2) MOA 1958 provides for notice to be given to the defendant, and to the person in whose favour the maintenance order was made, of the time and place appointed for consideration of the application. The non-attendance of either party does not preclude the court proceeding with the consideration of the application in their absence (s 18(7) MOA 1958). No form of notice is prescribed by the rules.

(b) Powers available to the court on review

The following powers are available to the court on review:

    (i)   remission of the arrears in whole or in part (s 18(3) and (6) MOA 1958); or

    (ii)   issue of the warrant (s 18(3) (a) MOA 1958); or

    (iii)   further postponement of the warrant until such time and on such conditions, if any, as the court thinks just (s 18(3)(b) MOA 1958); or

    (iv)   if in consequence of any change of circumstances of the defendant the court considers it appropriate to do so, an order that the warrant shall not be issued in any event (s 18(3)(c) MOA 1958).

(c) Remission

On considering an application referred to it by a single justice, a court may remit the whole or any part of the sum due under the order, in which case, either the order of commitment is discharged or the period of detention is reduced proportionately. Compliance, however, with MCR 1981 (notification to the person in whose favour the order is made etc) is not necessary since r 44 relates solely to the power of remission contained in s 95 MCA 1980 which applies before commitment (see page 60). The power to remit after commitment is contained in the MOA 1958 and no requirement similar to r 44 exists other than by way of natural justice. In any event the person in whose favour the order was made is required to be given notice of the time and place of the hearing, and could attend to make representations.

(b) Issue of the warrant

Even after hearing the defendant's application, the court may order the warrant of commitment to be issued forthwith. However, a substantial delay between the court giving notice of its intention to issue the warrant of commitment, and its actual issue, could result in the need for a fresh notice of intention to be served *(Slater* v *Calder Justices* (1984)). See page 152 for the prescribed form of warrant.

(c) Further postponement of the warrant

Clearly the court has wide powers to further postpone the issue of the warrant of commitment on such terms as it thinks just. However, if this course is followed the warrant cannot be issued without the process being commenced again. A further problem can arise if the court decides to adjourn the proceedings. Has it in fact postponed the issue of the warrant until another time (in which case the process must be started again), or are the same proceedings being continued? While a court has an unfettered discretion to adjourn any proceedings, it is submitted that in this situation, the court must adjourn only in exceptional circumstances, and in so doing clearly explain its intentions to the parties and record them in writing.

It should be noted that the court's power to order that the warrant shall not be issued in any event is only exercisable if there is a change in the circumstances of the defendant and only if the court considers it appropriate to do so. This precludes the court from going behind the original commitment decision.

8. Power to review where defendant already committed

(a) Application by defendant already committed

Any defendant who is already imprisoned or detained under a warrant issued for the enforcement of a maintenance order may make an application to the court, requesting that the warrant be cancelled and stating the grounds of his application (s 18(4) MOA 1958). Such an application cannot be made where the defendant is

Imprisonment for non-payment of maintenance

detained for some other reason. See page 154 for the prescribed form of application.

On the receipt of any such application, a justice of the peace may:

(i) refer it to the court if he is of the opinion that it should be further considered; or

(ii) if he is not of that opinion, refuse the application, in which case the defendant remains in custody and serves the remainder of the commitment.

A statement from solicitors on behalf of the defendant can be accepted as the disclosure of matters requiring further consideration *(Slater* v *Calder Justices* (1984)).

If the matter is referred to the court, the clerk must give notice to the defendant, the person entitled to receive payments and the person in charge of the prison or other place in which the defendant is detained of the time and place appointed for consideration of the application. The absence of any party to whom notice is required to be given does not preclude the court from proceeding with the consideration of the application. If the court is minded to remit the arrears in whole or part, additional compliance with r 44 MCR 1981 is not strictly necessary (s 18(7) MOA 1958). No form of notice is prescribed by the rules.

(b) Powers available to the court on review

The following powers are available to the court on review:

(i) remission of the arrears in whole or in part (s 18(5) and (6) MOA 1958); or

(ii) refusal of the application (s 18(5)(a) MOA 1958); or

(iii) where the court is satisfied that the defendant is unable to pay or to make any payment or further payment towards the sum outstanding, and it is of the opinion that in all circumstances the defendant ought not to continue to be detained under warrant, an order that the warrant shall cease to have effect when the person in charge of the prison (or other place) is informed of the making of the order (s 18(5)(b) MOA 1958).

If the court does order that the warrant shall cease to have effect, it may, if it thinks fit:

(i) fix a term of imprisonment in respect of the arrears remaining to be paid. The term must not exceed so much of the term of the previous warrant as remains to be served after taking account of any reduction occasioned by any of the arrears being remitted (s 18(5)(b)(i) MOA 1958); and

(ii) postpone the issue of a warrant for the commitment of the defendant for that term until such time and on such conditions, if any, as the court thinks just (s 18(5)(b)(ii) MOA 1958).

As with an application made before committal, further postponements of the warrant will result in the whole review procedure having to be followed again before issue. It is submitted that here also the court must not go behind the decision which resulted in the original order of commitment, but must confine itself to circumstances arising or becoming known since the original commitment.

(c) Notification to prison authorities

Where the court cancels the warrant of commitment, or remits the whole or any part of the sum in respect of which the warrant was issued, then the clerk must forthwith give written notice of the decision to the person in charge of the institution in which the defendant is detained (r 22(6) MC (MOA 1958) R 1959). No form of notice is prescribed.

Notice must be given to the person (if not present) in whose favour the maintenance order in question was made of any decision of the court pursuant to an application under either s 18(1) or s 18(4) MOA 1958 (r 22(5) MC (MOA 1958) R 1959).

Notice must also be given to the defendant if he was not present, except where an application under s 18(1) is dismissed. There is obviously little point in giving someone advance warning of their imminent arrest. No form of notice is prescribed.

9. Payment after imprisonment imposed

On payment of the full debt together with costs (if any), the commitment will cease to have effect, and the defendant will be released unless he is in custody for some other cause (s 79(1) MCA 1980).

Where payment is made of only part of the sum due, this will have the effect of reducing the period of detention proportionately even if this reduces the period of imprisonment to less than five days (s 79 MCA 1980). The persons authorised to receive part-payment after imprisonment has been imposed are prescribed by r 55 MCR 1981.

Chapter 7

Registration and enforcement of certain maintenance orders

1. Introduction

"Maintenance order" in this context means any order specified in sch 8 Administration of Justice Act 1970 (s 1(1A) and (2) MOA 1958); see page 49.

For the avoidance of any doubt the term also includes an order registered in a court in England and Wales under:

- Part II Maintenance Orders Act 1950;
- The Maintenance Orders (Facilities for Enforcement) Act 1920;
- Part I Maintenance Orders (Reciprocal Enforcement) Act 1972; or
- Part I Civil Jurisdiction and Judgments Act 1982.

In each case the order is deemed to be a maintenance order made by the court in which it is registered.

A High Court or county court order may be registered in a magistrates' court. A magistrates' court order may be registered in the High Court.

Neither a High Court order nor a magistrates' court order may be registered in a county court. However, a magistrates' court order registered in the High Court may still be enforced in the county court.

Whilst registered in the appropriate court, a maintenance order can be enforced in exactly the same manner as any order made by the court in which the order is registered. For example, an order registered in a magistrates' court under Part I Maintenance Orders Act 1958 is enforceable as a magistrates' court maintenance order (s 3(2) MOA 1958).

2. Registration of a High Court or county court order in the magistrates' court

(a) Application

Application for registration is to the court which made the order. That court has a discretion whether or not to allow registration (s 2(1) MOA 1958). A certified copy of the maintenance order and two copies of the application on Form No 115 (see page 155) must be lodged with the proper officer .

A Practice Direction issued in 1980 ([1980] 1 All ER 1007) by the President of the Family Division directed that applications for leave to register orders for nominal amounts in favour of spouses only should not be allowed, and, except in special circumstances, leave to register orders for maintenance pending suit and interim orders should not be granted.

Once the application to register is granted proceedings for the enforcement of the order before either registration or the expiration of the prescribed period (fourteen days in the High Court) (whichever occurs first) are prohibited (s 2(2) MOA 1958). The original court must, within the prescribed period, send a certified copy of the order, accompanied by a copy of the application for registration, to the clerk to the justices of the court in whose area "the defendant appears to be". The defendant need not "reside" in the area; he need only appear to be there. Consequently there seems to be no basis on which a court can refuse to accept registration if the address given is within the jurisdiction.

If, however, at the end of the prescribed period the original court has not been satisfied by the applicant that proceedings for enforcement have not been begun, the grant of the application to register becomes void. One interesting effect of this is that an attachment of earnings order, which becomes void on the grant of the application, remains void despite the application subsequently lapsing (s 116 Attachment of Earnings Act 1971).

On receiving a certified copy of the order the clerk of the magistrates' court registers the order by means of a memorandum entered and signed by him in the court register (r 4 MC (MOA 1958) R 1959). The clerk must send a notice to the High Court or county court confirming that the order has been so registered. Notice must also be given to the defendant that payments have become payable to the clerk of a magistrates' court (this need not necessarily be the court of registration). See page 156 for the prescribed form of notice to the defendant (r 5 MC (MOA 1958) R 1959).

Registration and enforcement of certain maintenance orders

(b) Enforcement of orders registered in the magistrates' court

A registered order is enforceable as a magistrates' court maintenance order in every respect as if it had been made in the court in which it is registered and as if that court had jurisdiction to make it (s 3(1), (2) and (4) MOA 1958). While it is registered no other proceedings for the enforcement of the order are possible. In *Smith* v *Smith* (1976) it was said that the magistrates' court should proceed to enforce an order even when an appeal is contemplated, unless the payer applies for and obtains a stay from the High Court or county court.

(c) Discharge of the order during or before registration

If the order remains or becomes registered after the discharge of the order the only enforcement proceedings possible are in relation to arrears which were due at the time of discharge (s 3(3) MOA 1958).

(d) Cancellation of registration

If the person entitled to receive payments under a registered order wishes the registration to be cancelled, notice may be given to the court of registration (s 5(1) MOA 1958). If that person is the clerk to the justices, notice cannot be given (presumably to himself in most cases) unless he has been requested in writing to do so by the person entitled to receive payments through him (s 20(1) MOA 1958). The clerk must comply with the request unless it appears to him to be unreasonable in the circumstances to do so.

In any proceedings taken by the clerk, it is the person who requested him to do so who is liable for costs, and not the clerk.

On the giving of notice to cancel registration, no proceedings for the enforcement of the registered order are to be begun before the cancellation of the registration (s 5(4)(a) MOA 1958). Furthermore no writ, warrant or other process for the enforcement of the order is to be issued in consequence of any such proceedings having been begun before the giving of the notice. Except where the defendant has already been detained in pursuance of the warrant, any warrant of commitment already issued for the enforcement of the order ceases to have effect once the person in possession of the warrant has been informed that notice has been given (s 5(4)(b) MOA 1958).

Registration of the order must be cancelled if the court of registration is satisfied by certificate that no process for the enforcement of the registered order, issued before the giving of the notice, remains in force, and that no proceedings for variation are pending in a magistrates' court (s 5(4) MOA 1958). See page 156 for the prescribed certificate that no enforcement or variation proceedings are pending.

On cancellation of registration the clerk must give notice to the High Court or county court, as the case may be, stating whether cancellation was in consequence of notice given by the person entitled to receive payments (r 7(3) and (5) MC (MOA 1958) R 1959). Proper notice is effected by a certified copy of the order being sent to the appropriate court stating, in the case of a High Court maintenance order, the title and cause number (if any); and in the case of a county court maintenance order, the plaint or application number (r 5(3) MC (MOA 1958) R 1959). Notice must also be given to the defendant and to the clerk of any court through which payments are being made. See page 157 for the prescribed form of notice to the defendant.

The clerk has a duty to record particulars of the cancellation in the court register and to notify any person who is in possession of a warrant of commitment which has not been executed (r 8 MC (MOA 1958) R 1959).

3. Registration of magistrates' court order in the High Court

(a) Application

A person entitled to receive payments under a magistrates' court order who considers that it could be more effectively enforced if it were registered in the High Court may apply for registration to the court which made the order (s 2(3) MOA 1958). The person "entitled to receive payments" could include a justices' clerk, but he may not apply for registration unless he is requested to do so in writing by the person entitled to recover payments through him (s 20(1) MOA 1958). On receiving such a request the clerk must comply with it unless it appears to him unreasonable in the circumstances to do so.

The application need not be in writing or on oath (r 1 MC (MOA 1958) R 1959), although it may be prudent for it to be so. The court may then, *if it thinks fit,* grant the application. While it used to be a requirement that arrears of at least four weekly payments (or at least two payments in the case of orders not payable weekly) existed before the court allowed registration, this is no longer the case.

It is possible to apply for the separate registration of a lump sum order where the person entitled to receive the lump sum considers that that sum could be more effectively enforced if registered in the High Court (s 2(3A) MOA 1958). Once again the court may, *if it thinks fit,* grant the application and, if it does, the lump sum is to be treated for the purpose of registration as if it were a separate order. It should be noted, however, that this is a specific provision to lump sums only; it does not provide a general ability to dissect orders and have different parts in different courts. Even if orders were considered in law to be divisible (which is doubtful) it would lead to much confusion in terms of paying, accounting and enforcing.

Once an application for registration in the High Court is granted, no proceedings for the enforcement of the order are to be begun before the registration takes place, and no warrant or other process for the enforcement of the order is to be issued in consequence of any proceedings begun *before* the start of the application (s 2(4)(a) MOA 1958).

Any warrant of commitment issued for the enforcement of the order ceases to have effect when the person in possession of the warrant is informed of the grant of the application, unless the defendant has already been detained in pursuance of the warrant (s 2(4)(b) MOA 1958).

The clerk must certify to the court that no process for enforcement remains in force before a certified copy of the order is sent to the proper officer of the High Court (s 2(4)(c) MOA 1958). See page 169 for the prescribed form of certificate that no process remains in force, and page 170 for the prescribed certificate that the order is a true copy.

On receipt of the certified copy the senior or district registrar must cause the order to be registered in the High Court by making an entry in the register or cause book and giving notice to the justices' clerk that the order has been duly registered. The details of the registration by the clerk must be entered in his register (s 8 MC (MOA 1958) R 1959).

Notice must also be given to the person liable to make payments that payment under the magistrates' court order (or an order made by a Sheriff's Court in Scotland, or a Court of Summary Jurisdiction in Northern Ireland) and registered in a magistrates' court under Part II MOA 1950 has, on its registration in the High Court, ceased to be payable to the clerk to the magistrates' court (r 5(2) MC (MOA 1958) R 1959). Where payments have been payable through a clerk other than the clerk of the administering court, a copy of the notice must be sent to that clerk. See page 170 for the prescribed form of notice that payments have ceased to be payable through the clerk of the magistrates' court.

(b) Enforcement of orders registered in the High Court

A magistrates' court order is enforceable in the High Court in all respects as if it had been made by the High Court and as if that court had the jurisdiction to make it (s 3(1) MOA 1958). While registered no other proceedings can take place.

It will, of course, be extremely rare for a magistrates' court order to be registered in the High Court. However, the High Court does have superior, and in some cases, unusual, powers (see *Thaha* v *Thaha* (1987)) which in some circumstances might be more appropriate. An example of this is where there is a very large lump sum order to enforce, or where the order, though deemed for the purpose of s 2A MOA 1958 to have been made by a magistrates' court in England, was in fact made in another part of the UK or in a country or territory outside the UK and interest can be claimed on the sum outstanding. For most people, however, there will be no practical advantage in a High Court registration.

(c) Cancellation

Cancellation is effected by the person entitled to receive payments (including the clerk to the justices if requested to do so in writing) giving notice to the appropriate officer of the High Court (s 5(1) and (4) MOA 1958). This will be either the senior registrar or a district registrar to whom a certified copy of the order has been sent pursuant to s 2(4)(c) MOA 1958. Once this has been done, no proceedings for the enforcement of the registered order can be commenced before the cancellation of the registration, and no writ, warrant or other process for enforcement can be issued in consequence of any proceedings begun before the giving of the notice.

The High Court, on being satisfied by affidavit that no process for enforcement remains in force, must then cancel the registration (RSC 1965 O 105 r 12). It must give notice to the clerk of the court which made the order (and where applicable to the clerk of the magistrates' court in which the order was registered in accordance with s 17(4) MOA 1950) stating, if such be the case, that cancellation was in consequence of a notice given by the person entitled to receive payments.

Registration and enforcement of certain maintenance orders

4. Registration of English orders in Scotland and Northern Ireland

(a) Orders which can be registered for enforcement

Registration is the only method of enforcing a maintenance order made by a court in England when the defendant resides in either Scotland or Northern Ireland (Part II MOA 1950). Parliament conveniently enacted that for legal purposes any reference to "England" was to include Wales, and, for the avoidance of doubt, Berwick-on-Tweed! (s 3 Wales and Berwick Act 1746.)

Any of the following orders made by a court in England may if registered be enforced in Scotland or Northern Ireland:

(i) an order made under ss 15–17, 19–22, 30, 34 and 35 Matrimonial Causes Act 1965, and ss 22, 23(1), (2) and (4) and s 27 Matrimonial Causes Act 1973;

(ii) an order made under Part I Domestic Proceedings and Magistrates' Courts Act 1978;

(iii) an order made under ss 11(B), 11c(1) or 11(D) Guardianship of Minors Act 1971, or s 2(3) or s 2(4A) Guardianship Act 1973;

(iv) an order made under s 47 Child Care Act 1980, or s 43 National Assistance Act 1948;

(v) an order made under s 18 Supplementary Benefits Act 1976;

(vi) an order made under s 34(1)(b) Children Act 1975 (s 16 MOA 1950).

(b) Procedure

In the case of a maintenance order made by a court of summary jurisdiction in England, application must be made by or on behalf of the person entitled to payments to a justice acting for the same place as the court which made the order (s 17 MOA 1950, and r 2(1) Maintenance Orders Act 1950 (Summary Jurisdiction) Rules 1950 ("MOA 1950 (SJ) R 1950"). Application may be made orally or in writing but unless the applicant appears in person a statutory declaration must be lodged by the applicant, with the clerk, containing the following:

(i) the address of the person liable to make payments under the order;

(ii) the reason why it is convenient that the order should be enforced in Scotland or Northern Ireland;

(iii) the amount of any arrears (only in cases where payments are not made through the clerk);

(iv) a declaration that the order is not already registered (r 2(2) MOA 1950 (SJ) R 1950).

No form of application is prescribed by the rules.

If it appears to the justice dealing with the application that the person liable to make payments resides in Scotland or Northern Ireland, and that it is convenient for the order to be enforced there, then the clerk of the court is to send to the appropriate officer of the court in Scotland or Northern Ireland the following:

(i) a certified copy of the order;
(ii) the certificate of arrears (see page 157 for the form) or statutory declaration (if any);
(iii) written notice of the address of the person liable to make payments (only if no statutory declaration has been lodged).

The appropriate officer will be, in Scotland, the sheriff clerk of the sheriff court which has jurisdiction in the area where the defendant appears to be; or, in Northern Ireland, the clerk of the court of summary jurisdiction having the same jurisdiction. Full details of courts in Scotland and Northern Ireland can be found in *Shaw's Directory of Courts in the United Kingdom,* and in cases of uncertainty the Home Office will provide the appropriate address on request. The list of addresses of sheriff clerks appended to Home Office Circular 241/1950 should no longer be relied upon.

When registered, notice of the registration is to be given by the appropriate officer in Scotland or Northern Ireland to the clerk of the magistrates' court which made the order, who, in turn, must cause details to be entered in his own register (s 17(4) MOA 1950 and r 2(4) MOA 1950 (SJ) R 1950).

It should be noted that while the defendant must *reside* in Scotland or Northern Ireland for the purpose of a justice determining whether registration should take place, the clerk need only send the particulars to the court having jurisdiction where the defendant "appears" to be. It is clear that Parliament intended the defendant's presence in either Scotland or Northern Ireland to have some degree of permanence, but how much is a matter of debate. "Residence" obviously indicates an address (which is confirmed by the rules), and it is submitted that this would be sufficient in most cases. However, it may well be that only a "care of" address or even a "box number" address is known, and in these cases "residence" is a question of fact and degree (see *R v Edgehill* (1963)).

As to the requirement that it should be convenient that the order be enforced in Scotland or Northern Ireland, if the applicant satisfies the justice concerned that the defendant is "resident" there, it is difficult to envisage when it would not be convenient to enforce there, particularly as it is the only remedy available to the applicant.

Where payments are made through the clerk of the court he must, if requested to do so by the person entitled to payments, make an application for registration on that person's behalf, but that person still remains liable for costs (s 17(6) MOA 1950).

The clerk is required to enter in the court register a memorandum of any proceedings taken in relation to an application for registration in Scotland or Northern Ireland, and on receipt of the notice of registration he must also cause particulars of that notice to be registered by means of a memorandum entered and signed by him in the register (s 17(5) MOA 1950 and r 2(4) MOA 1950 (SJ) R 1950).

(c) Re-registration of maintenance orders in Northern Ireland

Where a magistrates' court order has already been registered in a court of summary jurisdiction in Northern Ireland under Part II Maintenance Orders Act 1950, an application may be made to the court which made the order ("the original court") for its re-registration in the Northern Ireland High Court (s 36 Civil Jurisdiction and Judgment Act 1982). The court of summary jurisdiction in Northern Ireland is then unable to enforce the order so long as it is registered in another court. Re-registration in this manner is of value only where interest is recoverable.

(d) Enforcement of registered orders in Scotland or Northern Ireland

While registered, the order can be enforced in every respect by the court of registration as if that court had made the original order and had had jurisdiction to make it (s 18(1) MOA 1950). Parties seeking registration in Scotland should be made aware, however, that there are no collecting officers in Scotland and that it is not normal for the court itself to enforce the order. Legal aid may be available.

(e) The effect of registration

While an order is registered in either Scotland or Northern Ireland under Pt II MOA 1950 the following provisions apply:

(i) the order cannot be registered for enforcement in any other court (s 17(7) MOA 1950);
(ii) no proceedings for enforcement can be taken by any court in England (s 18(6) MOA 1950);
(iii) any provision in the order requiring payments to be made through the justices' clerk is of no effect as long as the order remains registered. The clerk is under a duty to notify the defendant by registered post or recorded delivery at his last known address that the payments through him have ceased to be so payable

(s 19(1) MOA 1950 and r 13(2) MOA 1950 (SJ) R 1950).

See page 157 for the prescribed form. Until he is given the prescribed notice the defendant is deemed to comply with the maintenance order if he makes payments in accordance with that maintenance order (s 19(4) MOA 1950).

(f) Cancellation

An application for the cancellation of registration may be made at any time to the clerk or sheriff clerk of the court in which the order is registered, by or on behalf of the person entitled to payments (s 24(1) and (2) MOA 1950). It is advisable that the application be in writing (stating the date of registration), enclosing a copy of the order the registration of which it is sought to cancel. Upon receiving such an application the clerk must cancel the registration and send written notice of the cancellation to the clerk of the court which made the order. On receipt of such notice that clerk must cause particulars of the same to be registered in his court by means of a memorandum. No form of application or notice is prescribed by the rules for use in Scotland or Northern Ireland.

An application for the cancellation of the registration may also be made, either orally or in writing, by or on behalf of the person *liable to make the payments,* to a justice acting for the same place as the court which made the order (s 24(2) MOA 1950). Unless the applicant attends in person he must lodge with the clerk a statutory declaration stating the facts upon which he relies in support of his application, namely that he has ceased to reside in Scotland or Northern Ireland as the case may be (r 5(1) and (2) MOA 1950 (SJ) R 1950). No form of application is prescribed by the rules.

If it appears to the justice dealing with an application that the person liable to make payments under the order has ceased to reside in either Scotland or Northern Ireland, he must have the clerk send notice of this to the clerk of the court in which the order is registered, who will then cancel the registration of the maintenance order (r 6 MOA (SJ) R 1950). Written notice of the cancellation must be sent to the clerk of the court which made the order and he must enter the particulars in the court register. Regardless of who the applicant was, notice of cancellation must be given to the person liable to make payments by the court cancelling the registration. Any provision in the original order requiring payments to be made to or through an officer of any court is revived (s 24(5) MOA 1950). However, until he receives notice of the cancellation, he is deemed to comply with the maintenance order if he makes payments in accordance with any order which was in force immediately before the cancellation. No forms for use in Scotland or Northern Ireland are prescribed by the rules.

5. Registration in England of maintenance orders made by courts in Scotland or Northern Ireland

(a) Orders which can be registered for enforcement

Part II Maintenance Orders Act 1950 provides fully reciprocal arrangements between courts in England, Scotland and Northern Ireland for the enforcement of maintenance orders made in those countries. Hence, just as English orders can be registered in Scotland or Northern Ireland, so too can orders from either of those countries be registered in England.

The following orders from Scotland can be registered in England: a decree for payment of aliment granted by a court in Scotland, including:

(i) an order for the payment of weekly or periodical sums under s 3(2) or 5(4) Guardianship of Infants Act 1925;

(ii) an order for the payment of sums in respect of aliment under s 1(3) Illegitimate Children (Scotland) Act 1930;

(iii) a decree for payment of aliment under s 44 National Assistance Act 1948 or s 26 Children Act 1948;

(iv) a contribution order under s 91 Children and Young Persons (Scotland) Act 1937, or an order under s 43 National Assistance Act 1948;

(v) an order for the payment of weekly or other periodical sums under s 11(3) Guardianship Act 1973;

(vi) an order made on an application under s 18 or s 19(8) Supplementary Benefits Act 1976;

(vii) a contribution order under s 80, or a decree or an order made under s 81 Social Work (Scotland) Act 1968;
(viii) an order of affiliation and aliment under s 24 Ministry of Social Security Act 1966

(s 16 MOA 1950).

An order for alimony, maintenance or other payments made by a court in Northern Ireland may be registered in England under or by virtue of any of the following enactments:

(i) Summary Jurisdiction (Separation and Maintenance) Act (Northern Ireland) 1945;
(ii) s 1 Illegitimate Children (Affiliation Orders) Act (Northern Ireland) 1924, s 21 National Assistance Act (Northern Ireland) 1948, s 12 Welfare Services Act (Northern Ireland) 1949, or s 124 Children and Young Persons Act (Northern Ireland) 1950;
(iii) s 122 Children and Young Persons Act (Northern Ireland) 1950, s 20 National Assistance Act (Northern Ireland) 1948, or s 11 Welfare Services Act (Northern Ireland) 1949;
(iv) any enactment of the Parliament of Northern Ireland containing provisions corresponding with ss 22(1), 34 or 35 Matrimonial Causes Act 1965; with ss 22, 23(1), (2) or (4) or s 27 Matrimonial Causes Act 1973; or with s 12(2) Guardianship of Minors Act 1971;
(v) s 24 or s 25 Supplementary Benefits Act (Northern Ireland) 1966;
(vi) Domestic Proceedings (Northern Ireland) Order 1980

(s 16 MOA 1950).

(b) Procedure

Application for the registration of an order in England must be made by or on behalf of the person entitled to payments, to the "appropriate authority". Where the maintenance order was made by a court of summary jurisdiction in Northern Ireland the appropriate authority is a resident magistrate acting for the petty sessions district of the court which made the order. In Scotland it is the prescribed officer of the court which made the order.

A statutory declaration or affidavit as to the amount of the arrears must accompany the application, and, in the case of payments made to or through an officer of the court (Northern Ireland only)

Registration and enforcement of certain maintenance orders

a certificate, also signed by that officer as to the amount of any arrears due under the order (s 20(1) MOA 1950).

If it appears to the appropriate authority that the person liable to make payments resides in England, and that it is convenient that the order should be enforceable there, the application must be granted and a certified copy of the order, together with the certificate, affidavit or statutory declaration, sent to the appropriate court in England (s 17(2) MOA 1950). This will be the High Court if the order to be registered was made by a superior court, and in all other cases the magistrates' court acting for the place in England where the defendant appears to be.

On receipt of the order the clerk must register it by means of a memorandum entered and signed by him in the court register (r 7 MOA Rules 1950). Notice has then to be sent to the court which made the order confirming that it has indeed been duly registered.

(c) Effect of registration

Every maintenance order registered under Part II MOA 1950 in a magistrates' court in England is enforceable as a magistrates' court maintenance order in all respects as if it had been made by that court and as if that court had jurisdiction to make it (s 18 MOA 1950). It follows therefore that enforcement proceedings cannot be taken by any other court in England except on behalf of the court of registration. However, the order can be registered in the High Court in England under Part 1 MOA 1958 but may not then be enforced under Part II MOA 1950 to the extent that it is for the time being registered (s 18(3A) MOA 1950).

While registered in England, the court of registration must, unless it is satisfied that it is undesirable to do so, order that all payments to be made under the maintenance order (including any arrears accrued before the date of registration) are to be paid through the court collecting officer, or the collecting officer of some other magistrates' court (s 19(2), (3) and (4) MOA 1950). However, until the person liable to make payments under the order is given notice to this effect, he is deemed to comply with the maintenance order if he makes payment in accordance with last existing instructions. See page 171 for the prescribed form of notice to the defendant.

(d) Cancellation

The procedure for the cancellation of a registration in England of an order made in Scotland or Northern Ireland is precisely the same as for the cancellation of the registration of an English order registered in Scotland or Northern Ireland; see page 86.

(e) English commitment warrants: execution in Scotland or Northern Ireland

Where a defendant moves to either Scotland or Northern Ireland after an English court has imposed a suspended period of imprisonment for the non-payment of maintenance, and that warrant falls to be issued, then the provisions of Part II MOA 1950 should not be required. This is because the Indictable Offences Act 1848 is applied to commitment warrants by s 126 of the Magistrates' Courts Act 1980. Therefore, provided the warrant is endorsed for execution in accordance with either s 12 or s 14 of the 1848 Act, the defendant should be arrested and brought back to England.

Chapter 8

Attachment of earnings

1. Introduction

An attachment of earnings order may be described as an instruction to an employer to make prescribed deductions from the earnings of a debtor, the amounts deducted being sent by the employer to the clerk of the court specified in the order.

Section 1 Attachment of Earnings Act 1971 ("AEA 1971") provides that a magistrates' court has power to make an attachment of earnings order to secure the recovery of any sum adjudged to be paid by a conviction or treated (by any enactment relating to the collection and enforcement of fines, costs, compensation, or forfeited recognizances) as so adjudged to be paid. This includes power to make such an order in respect of a legal aid contribution. Generally, a legal aid contribution order is treated as being enforceable as an affiliation order. For the purposes of attachment of earnings, however, this is not the case. All provisions relating to attachment of earnings to recover a sum adjudged to be paid by a conviction apply equally to a legal aid contribution order.

The court may also make an attachment of earnings order to recover payments under a maintenance order enforceable in a magistrates' court.

Earnings are defined as sums payable to a person:

(i) by way of wages or salary (including any fees, bonus, commission, overtime pay or other emoluments payable in addition to wages or salary payable under a contract of service);

(ii) by way of pension (including an annuity in respect of past services whether or not rendered to the person paying the annuity, and including periodical payments by way of compensation for the loss, abolition or

diminution in the emoluments, of any office or employment)
(s 24 AEA 1971).

The following are not to be treated as earnings:

(i) sums payable by any public department of the Government of Northern Ireland or of a territory outside the United Kingdom;

(ii) pay or allowances payable to the debtor as a member of HM Forces;

(iii) pension allowances or benefit payable under enactments relating to social security;

(iv) pension or allowances payable in respect of disablement or disability (but not "ill health" pensions: *Miles v Miles* (1979));

(v) wages payable to a person as a seaman other than wages payable to him as a seaman of a fishing boat.

2. Application and procedure

Except in relation to maintenance orders a court is not entitled to make an order of its own motion. It is a condition precedent to the making of an order that there should be proper application. A court dealing with an offender should not consider that it has power automatically to make an attachment of earnings order when it becomes apparent that an offender is employed. There is a formal procedure which must be followed.

Application for an order may be made:

(i) by the person to whom the payment under the relevant adjudication is required to be made (whether directly or through an officer of any court);

(ii) by the debtor;

(iii) in the case of a maintenance order under which payments are required to be made through the clerk of the court, by the clerk but only where he is requested to do so by the person entitled to payments. The request must be in writing and, where such a request is made, the clerk must comply with the request unless it appears to him unreasonable in the circumstances to do so (ss 3 and 18(1)(a) AEA 1971).

An application for an attachment of earnings order to secure

Attachment of earnings

maintenance payments cannot be made, except on the application of the debtor, unless at least fifteen days have elapsed since the making of the maintenance order.

As has been said above in regard to maintenance orders, the court is entitled to make an attachment of earnings order of its own motion. This applies where proceedings have been taken to enforce the maintenance order. The court may make an attachment of earnings order instead of dealing with the case by the issue of a warrant of distress or warrant of commitment, and in such a case no formal application is required.

Where an application is required, the application is by way of complaint (s 19(1) AEA 1971). No form of complaint is prescribed. The procedure to be adopted at the hearing is the same as for hearing complaints generally.

Where the application is made by the party to whom payment is required to be made, a summons should be issued to the debtor. Where application is made by the debtor, a summons should be issued to the person to whom payment is required to be made (whether directly or through an officer of any court (s 19(4) AEA 1971)).

A complaint for an order may be heard notwithstanding that it was not made within six months of the date when the matter of complaint arose (s 19(5) AEA 1971).

3. Power to obtain statement of earnings

Where a court has power to make an attachment of earnings order, it may order a debtor to give to the court within a specified period a statement signed by him of:

(i) the name and address of any person by whom earnings are paid to him;

(ii) specified particulars of his earnings and expected earnings and as to his resources and needs; and

(iii) specified particulars for the purpose of enabling the debtor to be identified by an employer of his

(s 14(1) AEA 1971).

In addition, the court may order an employer to give to the court within a specified period a statement, signed by him or on his behalf, of specified particulars of the debtor's earnings and expected earnings.

The power to require such a statement may be exercised by a

single justice or justices' clerk. It may be exercised before the hearing of the application or at any time after the attachment of earnings order has been made (s 14(2) AEA 1971). In the case of an application for the variation or discharge of an attachment of earnings order, such a statement can be ordered before the hearing of the application.

A document purporting to be a statement given in compliance with such an order is, in the absence of proof to the contrary, deemed to be a statement so given and is evidence of the facts stated therein (s 14(5) AEA 1971).

It is an offence not to comply with an order requiring a statement of earnings (s 23(2)(c) AEA 1971). It is an offence to make a statement purportedly in compliance with such an order knowing that it is false in a material particular, or to make a statement recklessly which is false in a material particular (s 23(2)(f) AEA 1971). In each case the maximum penalty on summary conviction is a fine not exceeding Level 2 on the standard scale (s 23(3) AEA 1971 and s 37 CJA 1982).

4. Power to make an order

(a) Application otherwise than by debtor

Before the court can make an order on the application of a person other than a debtor, it must appear to the court that the debtor has failed to make one or more of the payments required by the relevant adjudication (s 3(3) AEA 1971). Where payment by instalments has been allowed it may appear that although at some stage one or more payments were outstanding at the time they were required to be made, at the time of the hearing of the application for the attachment of earnings order, payments have been "brought up to date". In such circumstances an order can still be made.

In relation to maintenance orders, the court may not make an order if it appears that the debtor's failure to make payments under the maintenance order is not due to his wilful refusal or culpable neglect.

The debtor must be employed (s 6(2) AEA 1971). For the purposes of attachment of earnings the relationship of employer and employee exists between two persons if one of them, as a principal and not as servant or agent, pays to the other earnings (see page 91).

(b) Application by debtor

It is not necessary for the debtor to show that there has been a failure to make any of the required payments. There is nothing to prevent an application being made by the debtor immediately following a conviction or the making of an order. Such a step having much to recommend it, the court could helpfully remind a debtor that it is open to him to make the application.

5. The order

(a) Making the order

In making the order the court must:

(i) decide the amount of the normal deduction rate (s 6(5)(a) AEA 1971 and Sch 3 Part I). This is the sum to be deducted from the debtor's earnings after allowance has been made for income tax, superannuation contributions, contributions under Part III Social Security Act 1983, and contributions under Part I Social Security Act 1975. It is for the court to decide the size of the normal deduction and the period over which it should be made. It must ensure that the sum to be deducted is reasonable in all the circumstances, the deduction being made with reference to a week, month or other period.

In the case of an order to secure maintenance payments, the normal deduction rate is to be determined after taking into account any right or liability of the debtor to deduct income tax when making the payments; it must not exceed the rate which appears to the court necessary to secure the payments required under the maintenance order plus payment within a reasonable period of any outstanding arrears.

(ii) set what is called the *protected earnings rate* (s 6(5)(b) AEA 1971). This may be described as the level below which earnings actually paid to a debtor should not be reduced. In determining the level of the protected earnings rate, the court must take into account the debtor's resources and needs, including the needs of any person for whom he must, or reasonably may, provide. Should earnings on any pay-day be less than or equal to the protected earnings rate, the normal deduction should not be made (Sch 3 para 6(4) AEA 1971).

(b) Contents of order

Section 6 AEA 1971 and r 7 Magistrates' Courts (Earnings) Rules 1971 ("MC(E) R 1971") provide that the order must specify the normal deduction rate and the protected earnings rate. In addition, the order must:

(i) except where made to secure maintenance payments, specify the whole amount payable under the relevant adjudication (or so much of that amount as remains unpaid), including any relevant costs;

(ii) contain, so far as is known, the full name and address of the debtor, his place of work, the nature of that work, and his works number if any;

(iii) specify the court to which deductions made by the employer should be transmitted. In making an order the court may direct that deductions be sent to the court which made the order or to the clerk of such other court as may be specified.

Copies of the order must be served upon both employer and debtor (rr 6, 18 and 21 MC(E) R 1971). The employer should also be notified of the hours during which, and the place at which, payments are to be made and received. A copy of the order must also be given to the county court registrar for the district in which the debtor resides. See pages 158 and 159 for the prescribed form of order for maintenance and the prescribed form in respect of fines.

6. The employer

The employer's liability to make the deductions does not begin until seven days have elapsed since the service of the order (s 7(1) AEA 1971).

Where an employer is served with an order but he does not have the debtor in his employment, or the debtor subsequently ceases to be in his employment, he must within ten days from the date of service or cesser of employment, give notice of this to the court (s 7(2) AEA 1971). In addition, where a debtor leaves one employer and joins another, that other must notify the court in writing that he is the debtor's new employer and must include in his notification a statement of the debtor's earnings and expected earnings (s 15 AEA 1971). An employer will only have to do this, however, where he knows both that an order is in force and by what court it was made. The notification should be given within

Attachment of earnings

seven days of his becoming the debtor's employer or within seven days of his becoming aware of the order, whichever is later.

Any deductions made by an employer must be paid to the clerk of the court specified in the order (r 18 MC(E) R 1971). Any payment sent by post will be sent at the risk and expense of the employer.

The deduction required to be made by an employer on any pay-day is the specified normal deduction and is to be deducted as follows:

- (i) where it is a debtor's first pay-day, by reference to the period for which he is being paid, beginning with the first day of his employment;
- (ii) where it is not the first pay-day, then in a case where on the last pay-day payment was made in respect of a period falling wholly or partly after that pay-day, by reference to a period beginning with the first day after the period which payment has been made;
- (iii) in any other case, by reference to a period beginning with the first day after the last pay-day and ending:
  - where payment is made in respect of a period falling wholly or partly after the pay-day, with the last day of that period (this will cover such items as holiday pay);
  - in any other case, with the pay-day

(Sch 3 para 4 AEA 1971).

The protected earnings level is applied in the same way.

Before an employer is entitled to make the normal deduction, however, it must appear to him that attachable earnings on any pay-day exceed not only the protected earnings rate for the relevant period, but also any sum by which on previous pay-days attachable earnings fell short of the protected earnings rate that has not been made good by subsequent earnings. Where such a situation exists, then, once the shortfall in protected earnings has been made good by subsequent earnings, the normal deduction for the day in question, plus, in so far as the excess allows, so much of the normal deduction that on a previous pay-day was not deducted, can be made.

7. The debtor

While an order is in force the debtor must notify the court in writing of every occasion on which he leaves any employment, or becomes employed or re-employed, not later (in each case) than seven days from the date on which he did so (s 15 AEA 1971). In addition, the debtor must on any occasion when he becomes employed or re-employed, include in his notification particulars of his earnings and expected earnings.

8. Failure to comply with order

(a) The employer

An employer commits an offence if he fails to comply with an order, or fails to give the notices required above, or gives notice which he knows to be false in a material particular, or recklessly gives notice which is false in a material particular (s 23(2) AEA 1971). In addition, an employer commits an offence if, in purported compliance with the requirement to give such notice, he makes a statement which he knows is false in a material particular or recklessly makes a statement which is false in a material particular.

An employer who commits such an offence renders himself liable on summary conviction to a fine not exceeding Level 2 on the standard scale (s 23(3) AEA 1971 and s 37 CJA 1982).

(b) The debtor

A debtor commits an offence if he fails to give any notice required above, or gives a notice which he knows is false in a material particular, or recklessly gives a notice which is false in a material particular. He also commits an offence if, in purported compliance with any requirement above, he makes a statement which he knows is false in a material particular or recklessly makes such a statement.

A debtor who commits any such offence renders himself liable on summary conviction to a fine not exceeding Level 2 on the standard scale (s 23(3) AEA 971 and s 37 CJA 1982).

9. Variation and discharge

(a) General provisions

The court may make an order discharging or varying an attachment of earnings order (s 9 AEA 1971). The application is by way of complaint. It is not clear by whom such an application can be made. It is certainly not clear whether an employer is entitled to make it. It is submitted that the effect of s 19 AEA 1971 (procedure on applications) and s 51 MCA 1980 is to prohibit an employer from making such an application. Under s 51 AEA 1971 a justice may, on the making of a complaint, issue a summons to a person against whom an order can be made. Section 19 provides that for this purpose the power to make, vary or discharge an attachment of earnings order on the application of the debtor shall be deemed to be a power to make an order against the person to whom payment under the relevant adjudication is required to be made (whether directly or through an officer of the court), *and* the power to discharge or vary an attachment of earnings order on the application of any other person is deemed to be power to make an order against the debtor. Here it is submitted that the words "any other person" are limited to those persons against whom a summons could be issued and an order made on the application of the debtor. Hence an application for variation or discharge can be made by (i) the debtor or (ii) the person entitled to the payments.

There are no specific provisions about the matters to be taken into account by the court in deciding whether to vary or discharge an order. The court should therefore take into consideration such matters that it considers reasonable when dealing with such an application.

A copy of an order varying or discharging an attachment of earnings order must be served on the employer, the debtor and the county court (r 6 MC(E)R 1971).

No form of complaint is prescribed, nor any form of order of discharge or variation although there is a prescribed form of temporary variation (see below).

In the case of an order to secure maintenance payments, the clerk through whom payments are required to be made may not apply for the discharge or variation of the attachment of earnings order unless requested in writing to do so by the person entitled to receive payments (s 18(1)(b) and (c) AEA 1971). Where a request is made, the clerk must comply with the request unless it appears to him unreasonable in the circumstances to do so.

(b) Temporary variation

It is open to a debtor, where there has been a material change in his resources and needs since the order was made or last varied, to apply for a temporary variation of the protected earnings rate (s 9(3) AEA 1971 and r 14 MC(E) R 1971). It must be in writing setting out details of the changed circumstances. The application may be made to a single justice, or justices' clerk acting for the same petty sessions area as the court which made the order. No formal procedure is laid down. On being satisfied that there has been a material change in the debtor's circumstances, the justice or justices' clerk dealing with the application may by order vary the attachment of earnings order, by increasing the protected earnings rate for a period of not more than four weeks. A copy of the order for temporary variation must be served upon the employer. The order must be in the prescribed form (see page 160).

(c) Appropriate variation

In the case of an order made to secure maintenance payments, where it appears that:

(i) the aggregate of the payments made for the purposes of the maintenance order by the debtor (whether under the attachment of earnings order or otherwise) exceeds the aggregate of payments required up to that time by the maintenance order; and

(ii) the normal deduction rate exceeds the rate of payments required by the maintenance order; and

(iii) no proceedings for the variation or discharge of the attachment of earnings order are pending,

the clerk must apply to the court for the appropriate variation order. This is an order varying the attachment of earnings order by reducing the normal deduction rate to the rate of the payments required to be made by the maintenance order, or such lower rate as the court thinks fit having regard to any excess payment (s 10(1) AEA 1971). The court must grant such an application, unless the debtor appears and requests the court to discharge the order or to vary it in some other way, and the court thinks fit to grant the request. The clerk is required to give notice of the application to the person entitled to the payments under the maintenance order. The notice must be in writing setting out the time and place appointed for the hearing. The application is by way of complaint.

(d) Discharge and variation in respect of persons residing outside England and Wales

A magistrates' court has jurisdiction to hear a complaint by or against a person residing outside England and Wales for the discharge or variation of an attachment of earnings order made by a magistrates' court to secure maintenance payments (s 20(1) AEA 1971).

Attachment of earnings

Procedure is by way of complaint (s 20(3) and (4) AEA 1971). If the person summoned does not appear at the time and place appointed for the hearing of the complaint, the court may, if it thinks it reasonable in all the circumstances, proceed to hear the complaint in the absence of that party, provided it is proved to the satisfaction of the court that the complainant has taken steps to give notice to the defendant of the complaint, and of the time and place appointed for hearing the complaint (r 10(1) and (2) MC(E) R 1971). Any of the following steps, if proved to the satisfaction of the court, will suffice:

(i) the causing of written notice of the complaint and of the time and place appointed for the hearing to be delivered to the defendant;

(ii) the causing of written notice of the complaint and of the time and place appointed for the hearing to be sent by post, addressed to the defendant at his last known or usual place of abode, or at his place of business, or at some other address at which there is ground for believing that it will reach him;

(iii) the causing of notice of the complaint and of the time and place appointed for the hearing to be inserted in one or more newspapers on one or more occasions.

In relation to (i), the MCR 1981 apply for the purpose of proving delivery in the same way as they apply to prove service of a summons, with the addition that a declaration can also be made before a consular officer (r 67(1) MCR 1981 as modified by r 10(3) MC (E) R 1971). However, in relation to (ii) or (iii) the complainant must first apply for directions to the court dealing with the complaint, and the taking of such steps is only effective if they were taken in accordance with any directions given. Thereafter, any steps taken in relation to (ii) or (iii) can also be proved in accordance with the Magistrates' Courts Rules.

(e) Scotland and Northern Ireland

If the defendant resides in Scotland or Northern Ireland any process issued must be endorsed, in Scotland by a Sheriff, in Northern Ireland by a resident magistrate, and then served personally (r 67(1) MCR 1981 as modified by r 10(4) MC(E) R 1971). Service can then be proved by means of declaration before either of the above endorsing authorities, as the case may be. It follows therefore that the steps at either (ii) or (iii) above are not applicable (s 20(2) AEA 1971 and s 15 MOA 1950).

Whether a person is ordinarily resident is always a matter of fact and degree in each case (*R* v *Edgehill* (1963)).

(e) Debtor not traced

Where a complaint by the debtor for the variation or discharge of an attachment of earnings order is made against a person who does not appear at the time and place appointed for hearing the complaint then the court may, if it thinks it reasonable in all the circumstances, proceed to hear the complaint provided:

- (i) it is proved to the satisfaction of the court that the summons was served in accordance with r 99(1)(b) or (c) MCR 1981; and
- (ii) the complainant has caused notice of the complaint and of the time and place of the hearing to be inserted in one or more newspapers on one or more occasions (r 11(1) and (2) MC(E)R 1971).

It should be noted that the provisions of r 99(2) MCR 1981 (proof that the person had knowledge of the summons) are specifically dispensed with if the matters at (i) and (ii) above can be proved to the satisfaction of the court.

Application for directions must be made to the court before this procedure is used, and any other steps taken at (ii) are only effective if they comply with the directions given (r 67(2) MCR 1981 as modified by r 11(3) MC(E) R 1971). Thereafter any steps taken can be proved in accordance with MCR 1981.

10. Lapse and discharge

(a) Lapse

Where an order has been made and the employer ceases to have the debtor in his employment, the order lapses (except in regard to deductions from earnings paid after the cesser, and payment to the court of amounts deducted at any time) and is of no effect unless and until the court directs it to a person (whether the same as before or another) who appears to the court to have the debtor in his employment (s 9(4) AEA 1971).

Should an order so lapse, then if it appears to the court or justices' clerk that the debtor has subsequently entered the employment of a person (whether the same as before or another) the court may of its own motion vary the order by directing it to that person, and may make any consequential amendment to the order (s 9(3)(a)

Attachment of earnings

AEA 1971 and r 13 MC(E) R 1971). As the court proceeds by way of its own motion, no application is required.

The lapse of an order does not prevent its being treated as remaining in force for other purposes. This means, for example, that a debtor commits an offence if, where an order has lapsed, he becomes re-employed and fails to notify the court (see above).

(b) Discharge

Where it appears to a court or justices' clerk that the debtor is no longer employed, and that the likelihood of his entering the employment of any person is not such as to justify preserving the order the court may, of its own motion, discharge the order (r 13 MC(E)R 1971). Where the court so discharges an order, the employer is under no liability in consequence of his treating it as still in force at any time before the expiration of seven days from the date on which a copy of the discharging order is served on him (s 12(3) AEA 1971).

11. Power of court to determine whether payments are earnings

Where an order is in force, the court has power, on application, to decide whether payments to a debtor of a type specified in the application are earnings for the purposes of the order. The application to the court is by way of complaint. No form of complaint is prescribed. An application for such a determination may be made by:

(a) the employer;
(b) the debtor;
(c) the person to whom payment under the relevant adjudication is required to be made (whether directly or through an officer of any court)

(s 16 AEA 1971).

Once a determination has been made an employer is entitled to give effect to it.

Where application has been made by an employer, he does not incur any liability for non-compliance with the order in respect of any payments of the class specified in the application while the application or any appeal in consequence thereof is pending. This ceases to apply, unless the court otherwise directs, if the employer subsequently withdraws the application or abandons the appeal.

The court may make such order as it thinks just and reasonable for the payment by any of the parties to the application of the whole or any part of the costs of the determination (s 21 AEA 1971).

12. Consolidated orders

The power to make an attachment of earnings order includes the power to make an order to secure the discharge of any number of relevant liabilities. An order made in this manner is known as a consolidated attachment of earnings order (r 15 MC(E) R 1971). Thus, rather than make a number of orders, the court may instead make one consolidated order.

This power is extended as follows:

    (a) in a case where the court has power to make an attachment of earnings order in respect of a debtor who is already subject to such an order made by any magistrates' court, the court may discharge the existing order and make a consolidated order in respect of the debtor;

    (b) where two or more orders (whether or not themselves consolidated orders) made by magistrates' courts are in existence in respect of a debtor, any such court may discharge the existing orders and make a consolidated order.

A court is not, however, entitled under either (a) or (b) to discharge an existing order made by another magistrates' court without first giving notice to the clerk of that court. In addition, enforcement of the sum to which the other order related must first be transmitted to the court wishing to make the consolidated order. Transfer of enforcement in such circumstances may be by way of the normal provisions relating to transfer of fines (r 16 MC(E) R 1971; see page 4). Where a court wishes to make a consolidated order and the debtor does not reside within the petty sessions area for which that court acts, nor is within the area of the court which made the existing attachment of earnings order, then the court which made the existing order may make an order transferring enforcement of the sum to which the order relates to the court wishing to make the consolidated order.

The power to make a consolidated order may be exercised by the court of its own motion or on the application of the debtor.

It is open to an employer to apply in writing to the clerk of the court which has power to make a consolidated order, requesting the court to make such an order (r 15(7) MC(E) R 1971). The clerk must then bring the application before the court. If it appears to the court that the application is justified, it proceeds as if it had determined of its own motion to make such an order.

Where the court proceeds by way of its own motion in a case to which (b) above applies, the court must send written notice to the debtor informing him of his right to make representations to the court before it exercises its power (r 15(8) MC(E) R 1971).

The debtor's application for a consolidated order may be made at the hearing of the proceedings for the enforcement of the fine or other liability both where the court has power to make an original consolidated order and where this power is extended as in (a) above. In cases to which (b) applies the debtor's application is by way of complaint.

Payments received under a consolidated order are to be applied first against sums previously secured by an attachment of earnings order subsequently discharged in consequence of the making of the consolidated order (r 17 MC(E) R 1971). Where two or more such attachment of earnings orders have been discharged the sums due under these orders must be paid off chronologically.

On making a consolidated order the court may set the normal deduction rate at such level as it thinks reasonable, which may be less than the sum of the normal deduction rates specified in the attachment of earnings orders discharged by the court (r 15(10) MC (E) R 1971).

13. Cessation of order

An order ceases to have effect upon the issue of a warrant committing the debtor to prison for default in making the payment of the sum to which the order related (s 8(5) AEA 1971). In the case of an order made to secure maintenance payments, the order ceases to have effect as follows:

(a) on the making of an order of commitment or the issue of a warrant of commitment in proceedings for enforcement of the maintenance order, and where the court postpones the issue of the warrant of commitment in such proceedings;

(b) upon the grant of an application for registration in a magistrates' court of a High Court or county court maintenance order, or upon the grant of an application for registration in the High Court of a magistrates' court maintenance order;

(c) upon the discharge of the maintenance order while it is not registered as above, provided that where there remain arrears to be recovered after the maintenance order is discharged, the court discharging the order may direct that the attachment of earnings order should not cease by virtue of the discharge of the related maintenance order.

Where an order ceases to have effect in such circumstances, notice of the cesser must be given to the employer by the clerk of the court which issued the warrant of commitment (s 12(1) AEA 1971 and r 21 MC(E) R 1971). A copy of the notice must be given to the county court registrar for the district in which the debtor resides. The employer is under no liability in consequence of his treating the order as still in force at any time before the expiration of seven days from the date on which the notice was served upon him.

14. Priority between orders

Where an employer has to comply with two or more orders made by a magistrates' court in respect of one debtor, then on any pay-day the employer must:

(a) deal with the orders according to the dates on which they were made, disregarding any later one until an earlier one has been dealt with; and

(b) deal with any later order as if the earnings to which it relates were the residue of the debtor's earnings after the making of any deduction to comply with any earlier order

(Sch 3 para 7 AEA 1971).

When one or more (but not all) of the orders have been made to secure payment of a judgment debt or administration order, then on any pay-day the employer must:

(a) deal first with any order made by a magistrates' court as above: and

(b) deal thereafter with any order not made by a magistrates' court in the same way as orders made by magistrates' courts

(Sch 3 para 8 AEA 1971).

15. Service of orders and notices

Where a court makes an attachment of earnings order or makes or discharges such an order, the clerk must ensure that a copy of the order is served upon the employer and the debtor (rr 6 and 21 MC(E) R 1971). A copy of the order must be given to the county court registrar for the district in which the debtor resides.

Any notice or order required to be served on the debtor may be served by delivering it to him personally, or by sending it by post to him at his last known or usual place of abode (r 20 MC(E) R 1971).

Any notice or order required to be served on the employer may be served, in the case of a corporation, by delivering the document or by sending it to its registered office if this is in England or Wales. If other than a corporation, service may be effected at any place where the corporation trades or conducts its business; or by delivering or sending the document to such office or place as the corporation may have specified in writing to the court in relation to the debtor or in relation to a class or description to which he belongs. In the case of an employer who is not a corporation, service may be effected by delivering or sending the document to his place of business.

Chapter 9

Enforcement of legal aid contribution orders

1. Introduction

Legal Aid regulations (SI 1983 No 1963) made by the Lord Chancellor, which came into effect on 1 March 1984, made substantial changes in the arrangements for ordering, determining and collecting legal aid contributions in criminal proceedings.

When an application for legal aid is made, contributions are assessed and prescribed figures for income and capital are taken into account in assessing a defendant's resources. Those with disposable income or capital levels below the prescribed limit (the "free limit") pay no contribution from income or from capital.

Where a contribution *is* ordered, it is to be paid in instalments from the date on which legal aid is granted. The instalments fall due weekly, but can be collected fortnightly or monthly should the court and the defendant find this more convenient.

The regulations also provide for re-assessment where an assisted person's resources change, and for consequent variation of the contribution order. If the assisted person wilfully refuses to pay instalments, the courts have power, during the proceedings, to revoke legal aid if satisfied that the assisted person could afford to pay at the time he fell into arrears and can currently afford to pay all or part of the sum. He must, however, have been given the opportunity to make representations against revocation. It may be preferable to use the normal methods of enforcement at the end of the proceedings. At the conclusion of the case, the court before which the proceedings have been held has the power to remit any or all of the contribution instalments which have *not* fallen due, and to return contributions to acquitted defendants.

2. Recovery by the collecting court

Section 35(1) and (8) Legal Aid Act 1974 ("LAA 1974") provide that any sum ordered to be paid after 1 August 1971 by way of a legal aid contribution order is recoverable by the collecting court as if it had been adjudged to be paid by an order of that court. "Collecting court" means a magistrates' court specified in the order, namely:

- (i) where the court making the order is itself a magistrates' court, that court;
- (ii) where the order is made on appeal from a magistrates' court, or in respect of a person who was committed (whether for trial or otherwise) to the Crown Court, the court from which the appeal is brought or, as the case may be, which committed him; and
- (iii) in any other case, a magistrates' court nominated by the court making the order

(s 32(s) LAA 1974).

Any provision made by the court which made the order as to time for payment, or payment by instalments, is treated as made by the collecting court (Sch 3 para 2 LAA 1974).

3. Commencement of proceedings

Section 9(2) Legal Aid Act 1982 ("LAA 1982") provides that any sum due under a legal aid contribution order cannot be recovered, and payment of any such sum cannot be enforced, until either the conclusion of the relevant proceedings, or the revocation of the legal aid order in connection with which the legal aid contribution order was made.

Usually, however, the legal aid contribution order will not be enforced until the conclusion of the relevant proceedings. It will be rare for the court to revoke legal aid during the proceedings and enforce the contributions outstanding at the time of revocation.

Courts are advised to delay enforcing a contribution order until notification of the taxed costs is received from the taxing authority, in case repayment of any contribution in excess of the taxed costs is required. Unfortunately this can and does delay enforcement for several weeks.

4. Procedure for recovery

Various provisions apply as if a legal aid contribution order were enforceable as a magistrates' court maintenance order. They have been examined in full earlier but for the sake of completeness the following is a brief summary of the essential provisions:

- (a) proceedings are begun by complaint;
- (b) a complaint must not be made earlier than the fifteenth day after the making of the order;
- (c) the court must not hear the complaint in the absence of the defendant, unless it is proved to the satisfaction of the court that the summons was served on him within a reasonable time before the hearing, or the defendant has previously appeared;
- (d) an attachment of earnings order can be made (even for sums due before 2 August 1971);
- (e) a warrant may be issued for the arrest of the defendant if the complaint is substantiated on oath;
- (f) instead of requiring immediate payment, the court can allow time for payment or order payment by instalments;
- (g) imprisonment for default must not be imposed unless the court has inquired, in the defendant's presence, as to whether the default was due to the defendant's wilful refusal or culpable neglect, and the court is of the opinion that it is so due;
- (h) imprisonment for default must not be imposed unless the court is of the opinion that it is inappropriate to make an attachment of earnings order;
- (i) imprisonment for default must not be imposed in the absence of the defendant;
- (j) a warrant of commitment must comply with Sch 4 MCA 1980 regarding maximum periods of imprisonment, but in any event must not exceed six weeks;
- (k) imprisonment does not operate to discharge the defendant from liability to pay the sum in respect of which he has been committed;
- (l) a defendant cannot be committed more than once in respect of the same arrears;
- (m) any moneys found on the defaulter can be applied to satisfy the debt;
- (n) the court has the power to review committals, and the provisions of s 18 MOA 1958 apply as if the legal aid contribution order were a maintenance order;

(o) the court has the power to remit arrears;
(p) any costs awarded on the enforcement of a legal aid contribution order are enforceable as part of that order.

5. Transfer of enforcement proceedings to a different court

Where it appears to the collecting court that a person subject to a legal aid contribution order is residing in another petty sessions area, it may make an order making payments under the legal aid contribution order enforceable in that other petty sessions area (Sch 3 para 7 LAA 1974). This order is referred to as a "transfer order".

6. Members of the armed forces

Where a legal aid contribution order has been made in respect of a member of the armed forcesand deductions are being made by the Secretary of State from that person's pay, the court cannot enforce the order unless and until the Secretary of State has notified it that the person is no longer a member of the forces (s 35(4) LAA 1974).

7. Recovery in the High Court or county court

A legal aid contribution order is enforceable in the High Court or county court (otherwise than by issue of a writ of *fieri facias* or other process against goods, or by imprisonment, or attachment of earnings) as if the sum were due to the clerk of the collecting court by a judgment or order of the High Court or county court (s 35(2) and (5) LAA 1974). However, no proceedings for recovery may be taken in the High Court or county court by the clerk unless he is authorised to do so by the court.

8. Costs of a legally aided person paid by any other person

Where a court makes an order that the costs of a legally aided person are to be paid by any other person, the clerk to the justices must notify the Law Society of the order and of the name and address of the person by whom the costs are to be paid. Where a person ordered to pay the costs of a legally aided person does not pay them, they may be recovered summarily by the Law Society, as a sum adjudged to be paid as a civil debt by order of a magistrates' court (rr 27 and 28 Legal Aid Criminal Proceedings (General) Regulations 1968).

Chapter 10

Civil debt

1. Introduction

Rather confusingly the subject of civil debt is divided into two areas; those sums which are *recoverable* as a civil debt, and those which are *enforceable* as a civil debt.

2. Sums recoverable as a civil debt

(a) Generally

A magistrates' court has power, on complaint, to make an order for the payment of any money recoverable summarily as a civil debt. Any sum ordered by a magistrates' court is recoverable summarily as a civil debt, except the following:

(i) a sum recoverable on complaint for a magistrates' court maintenance order; or
(ii) a sum that may be adjudged to be paid by a summary conviction or by an order enforceable as if it were a summary conviction (s 58(1) and (2) MCA 1980).

(b) Procedure

Application is by complaint to the court which has jurisdiction in the area where the act was either done or left undone (in this case where the debt is payable) and the defendant is to be summoned (ss 51 and 52 MCA 1980). Complaint must be made within six months from the time the matter of complaint arose, namely when the debt became due (s 127 MCA 1980), but note the *twelve* month time limit allowed for the recovery of any tax charged under Schedule E (s 65(3) Taxes Management Act 1970).

See page 160 for the prescribed form.

(c) Hearing

On hearing the complaint, the substance of it is to be stated to the defendant if he appears. After hearing the evidence and the parties, the court must make the order or dismiss the complaint. With the consent of the defendant the court may make the order without hearing the evidence (s 53 MCA 1980). Otherwise the order of evidence and speeches is as prescribed by MCR 1981.

Procedures regarding adjournments and non-appearance of either the defendant or the complainant are governed by the general provisions contained in Part II MCA 1980 relating to civil jurisdiction and procedure, in particular s 54 (adjournments); s 55 (non-appearance of defendant); s 56 (non-appearance of complainant); and s 57 (non-appearance of both parties). The court, however, is precluded from issuing a warrant for the arrest of the defendant if he fails to appear (s 55(8)).

(d) The order

A sum "recoverable as a civil debt" simply means a sum which has not yet been, but may be, ordered to be paid; the order therefore is for payment of the debt. All the court has to satisfy itself is that the debt is indeed a civil debt, and that it is owed by the defendant. Any question of wilful refusal or culpable neglect is irrelevant. However, the court is not obliged to make the order and could, with good cause, decline to do so. Bankruptcy, however, does not appear to be good cause since a bankruptcy notice may be founded on the making of a civil debt order *(Re A Debtor (No 48 of 1952), ex parte Ampthill Rural District Council* v *The Debtor* (1953)). See page 161 for the prescribed form of order. The court may order immediate payment of the money or allow payment by instalments; it may even allow further time to pay (s 75 MCA 1980).

Default by the defendant in paying one instalment renders the whole amount enforceable. In *Abley* v *Dale* (1851) and *ex parte Kinning* (1847) it was suggested that where time for payment is allowed in relation to the payment of a civil debt, then before further process is issued for the enforcement of such a debt, the defendant should be given the opportunity of being heard. The principle appears to be that, notwithstanding the defendant's non-payment, circumstances might possibly occur between the making of the order and the time of imprisoning the defendant which would cause the judge not to commit him. In *ex parte Kinning*, Maule J said: "suppose, for instance, the man were in the last stage of cholera when the time for payment arrives; should he not have

Civil debt

an opportunity of making that fact known to the judge before being committed for non-payment".

While accepting that today it would be rare for a defendant to be "in the last stage of cholera" the principle behind the judgment is still as relevant. The very object of the order is to make the payments subject to all the contingencies which may happen at a future time. As a rule of practice, if nothing else, it is strongly suggested that a summons should be issued before further action is taken.

(e) Reserve and auxiliary forces

Protection is available to members of the reserve and auxiliary forces. Leave to proceed may be required in accordance with the Reserve and Auxiliary Forces (Protection of Civil Interests) Rules (SI 1951 No 1401).

(f) Costs

Costs are payable at the discretion of the court in such amount as it thinks just and reasonable (s 64(1) MCA 1980), but the complainant's costs can only be paid on making the order for which the complaint is made. Similarly, the defendant's costs can only be paid on dismissing the complaint.

Costs ordered to be paid are *enforceable* as a civil debt.

3. Sums enforceable as a civil debt

A sum enforceable as a civil debt means:

(i) any sum recoverable summarily as a civil debt *which is adjudged to be paid by the order of a magistrates' court;*

(ii) any other sum expressed by the MCA 1980 or any other Act to be so enforceable (s 150 MCA 1980). In the case of a sum expressed by the MCA 1980 or any other act to be enforceable as a civil debt, no "civil debt order" made as a result of civil debt proceedings is required before enforcement is commenced. For example, costs ordered in civil proceedings under s 64 MCA 1980 (subject to exceptions) are described as being "enforceable as a civil debt".

The powers available to the court in enforcing civil debt are distress (available in all cases) or imprisonment (restricted to a very few cases).

4. Distress

A distress warrant is not to be issued for failure to pay a sum of money enforceable as a civil debt unless:

(i) a copy of the minute of the order has been served by delivering it to the defendant or by sending it to him by post at his last known or usual place of abode; or

(ii) the order was made in his presence and the warrant issued on that occasion

(r 53 MCR 1981).

For the general procedure in issuing a distress warrant see Chapter 1.

5. Imprisonment

(a) Generally

The Administration of Justice Act 1970 severely restricted the magistrates' powers to commit for civil debt. They can now only commit in relation to orders for the payment of the following:

(i) income tax or any other tax liability recoverable under s 65, 66 or 68 Taxes Management Act 1970 (provided the sum is less than £250);

(ii) selective employment tax under s 44 Finance Act 1966;

(iii) Reserve Scheme contributions and premiums under Part III Social Security Act 1973;

(iv) Class 1, 2 and 4 contributions under Part I Social Security Act 1975;

(v) redundancy funds contributions under s 27 Redundancy Payments Act 1965

(s 12 and Sch 4 Administration of Justice Act 1970).

Restrictions in relation to the custody of young persons imposed by the Criminal Justice Act 1982 are also applicable (s 96A MCA 1980).

(b) Procedure

Application is by complaint and can be made at any time, notwithstanding the normal six months' time limitation (s 96 MCA 1980).

Proceedings for the summary recovery of any tax due will be

Civil debt

commenced in the name of a collector and proceedings begun by one collector may be continued by another (s 1(3) Taxes Management Act 1970). All or any of the sums due in respect of tax from any one person and payable to any one collector may, whether or not they are due under one assessment, be included in the same complaint, summons, order, warrant or other document; and every such document shall be construed as a single document as respects each sum (s 65(2) Taxes Management Act 1970).

The summons is known as a "judgment summons" and must be served on the judgment debtor personally (r 58 MCR 1981). However, if a justice of the peace is satisfied by evidence on oath that prompt personal service is impracticable he may allow the summons to be served in such a way as he thinks just in the circumstances of that particular case. Service of the summons outside the commission area can be proved by affidavit, although the Summary Jurisdiction (Process) Act 1881 (Service of Process in Scotland) does not apply to the recovery of civil debts. See pages 162 and 163 for the prescribed forms of complaint and summons.

Where the summons was served less than three clear days before the hearing, the court may not hear the complaint unless the judgment debtor actually appears and consents to an immediate hearing.

If the defendant fails to appear at the time and place appointed for the hearing, the court can proceed in his absence (s 55(1) and (8)). A warrant cannot be issued for the debtor's arrest in proceedings for the enforcement of a sum recoverable summarily as a civil debt, nor can a warrant for the arrest of a witness (ie the debtor) be issued as an indirect method of procuring attendance (s 97(2) MCA 1980).

(c) The hearing

The complainant must prove to the satisfaction of the court that:

(i) the judgment debtor has, or has had since the date on which the sum was adjudged to be paid, the means to pay the sum, or any instalment of it on which he has defaulted; and

(ii) he refuses or neglects, or has refused or neglected to pay it

(s 96(1) MCA 1980).

While the court is under no statutory obligation to consider all other methods, it must surely be the case that imprisonment is to be used only as a last resort where no other method is appropriate. Where there is a reasonable likelihood that the debtor has assets available to satisfy the debt the justices should proceed by way of distress rather than by commitment (see *R* v *Birmingham Justices, ex parte Bennett* (1983) and *R* v *Norwich Justices, ex parte Tigger (formerly Lilly)* (1987) concerning the use of distress warrants in other circumstances).

The court has no power to make a money payment supervision order or remit any part of the civil debt.

(d) Period of imprisonment

The maximum periods applicable are those contained in Sch 4 MCA 1980 but must not in any event exceed six weeks; see page 27. Postponement of the warrant is possible but it may not be issued, it is submitted, without giving the defendant the right to be heard (see *R* v *Colchester Justices, ex parte Wilson* (1985), and page 5). See page 164 for the prescribed form.

(e) Payment after imprisonment imposed

On payment of the full debt together with costs (if any) the commitment will cease to have effect, and the defendant will be released unless he is in custody for some other cause (s 79(1) MCA 1980).

Where payment is made of only part of the sum due, this will have the effect of reducing the period of detention proportionately even if the period of imprisonment is reduced to less than five days (s 79 MCA 1980). The persons authorised to receive part payment after imprisonment has been imposed are being prescribed by r 55 MCR 1981.

(f) Attachment of earnings

There is no provision for a magistrates' court to make an attachment of earnings order in relation to civil debt (ss 1 and 2 AEA 1971). However, the county court can make an attachment of earnings order to secure the payment of a judgment debt not less than £5. This would include a magistrates' court order which is enforceable as a civil debt.

(g) Costs

The court may order the debtor to pay such costs as it thinks just and reasonable (s 64 MCA 1980). Where the defendant is committed to custody, such costs incurred by the complainant as the court may direct shall be included in the sum on payment of which the defendant may be released from custody (s 96(3) MCA 1980).

Chapter 11

General rates

1. Introduction

The power to enforce payment of rates derives from s 96 General Rate Act 1967 ("GRA 1967"). By this section, should any person fail to pay a sum legally assessed and due from him in respect of a rate, for seven days after it has been legally demanded, payment of the sum may be enforced in accordance with the provisions of the Act, by distress, and, in the event of insufficient distress, imprisonment. The Magistrates' Courts Act 1980 does not apply to the recovery of rates. The six month limitation period on bringing actions contained in s 127 will not therefore apply. Note that when the rates are replaced by the community charge, the provisions for enforcement will doubtless be modified.

2. Distress

(a) Application for warrant of distress

The application is by way of complaint (s 97(1) GRA 1967). In the first instance application is made for a summons to be issued to the person named in the complaint, requiring him to appear before the court to show why the rate has not been paid. Should the person named in the summons fail to appear, and it is proved to the court on oath or by certificate of service in accordance with r 67 MCR 1981, that the summons was served a reasonable time before the hearing, the court may, if it thinks fit, proceed in his absence (s 97(3) GRA 1967). See pages 165 and 166 for the prescribed forms of distress warrant.

(b) Service of summons

A summons issued in accordance with the above provisions may be served as follows:

General rates

(i) by delivering it to the person; or
(ii) by leaving it at his usual or last known place of abode, or in the case of a company at its registered office; or
(iii) by post addressed to the person at his usual or last known place of abode, or in the case of a company at its registered office. Service by post is not required to be by way of registered or recorded delivery post; or
(iv) by delivering it to some person on the premises to which it relates; or
(v) where the property to which the summons relates is a place of business of the person to whom it is to be served, by leaving it at or forwarding it by post addressed to the person at the place of business. Again service by post is not required to be by way of registered or recorded delivery post.

See pages 164 and 165 for the prescribed forms of complaint and summons.

(c) Hearing

The court must be composed of at least two justices, except where a stipendiary magistrate is authorised to act (s 106 GRA 1967).

Application will be made for the court to issue a warrant of distress against the person named in the complaint. It is for the rating authority to show that the person against whom the proceedings are taken is a person who has failed to pay a sum legally assessed on and due from him in respect of a rate for seven days after it has been legally demanded. Evidence of the making and publication of the rate may be given by certificate (s 10(1) GRA 1967).

(d) Objection

Objection to the proceedings can be raised at the hearing of the application for the warrant of distress. In *Shillitoe* v *Hinchcliffe* (1922) the court outlined the approach to be followed when dealing with objections to rateability:

"... does the objection taken amount to an allegation (i) that the rating authority have acted in excess of their jurisdiction? or (ii) that they have acted erroneously in the exercise of their jurisdiction? If the objection belonged to the former class, it could be raised when application was made for the distress warrant; if it belonged to the latter class, it could not".

However, in *Verrall* v *Hackney London Borough Council* (1983) the court overturned what seemed to be an established principle that the question of who was in rateable occupation was not one for magistrates to decide. It was held in this case that a magistrate hearing a summons for the issue of a distress warrant for non-payment of rates had jurisdiction to investigate whether the person summoned was in occupation of the relevant hereditament. It was said that the cases which had established the existing principle were wrongly decided and should not be followed.

The question of husband and wife is one that often causes anxiety. What is the position when the husband leaves the matrimonial home? In *Locker* v *Stockport Metropolitan Borough Council* (1984) it was held that a wife, who remained in occupation of the matrimonial home after her husband had separated from her and who had not brought any matrimonial proceedings against her husband, was an occupier for the purposes of the GRA 1967 by reason of her actual occupation of the matrimonial home coupled with her continuing legal rights of joint ownership. In *Doncaster Metropolitan Borough Council* v *Lockwood* (1987) it was held that a husband who had separated from his wife and left the matrimonial home was not necessarily liable for rates on the home before the pronouncement of the decree absolute. This was possible even though the house remained in his name or in the joint names of both spouses, where on the facts the husband had left the home and the separation was so complete that the husband no longer had any responsibility for the wife.

It appears from these cases that where a wife continues in actual occupation of the former matrimonial home after her husband has left, then if the husband has shown that he has no responsibility for her, she is liable to pay rates whether or not matrimonial proceedings have been instituted.

It has further been established that a receiver appointed by a debenture holder, with power to take possession of property and to manage a company's business, was to be rated as an agent of the company and under no personal liability for rates *(Ratford and Hayward* v *Northavon District Council* (1986)). Where a rating *authority* has applied the provisions of s 17 and Sch 1 para 1 then the three month exemption from rates in respect of unoccupied property was not affected by a change of ownership during the three months, and that the new owner was not entitled to a further rate free period *(Camden London Borough Council* v *Bromley Park Gardens Estates Ltd* (1985)).

Unless an objection is made out, the court must issue the warrant (s 99 GRA 1967). There is no power to refuse. A warrant of distress issued in accordance with these provisions may be directed

General rates

to the rating authority, to the constables of the police area in which the warrant is issued, and to such other persons, if any, as the court issuing the warrant think fit. The warrant authorises the persons to whom it is directed to levy the amount which the person against whom the warrant is issued is liable to pay, by distress and sale of his goods and clothes.

(e) Costs and charges for distress

On the issue of a warrant of distress the court may, if it thinks fit, include in it an order that such sum as it may deem reasonable for the costs incurred in obtaining the warrant shall be levied under the warrant (s 100 GRA 1967). This is subject to the restriction that where several rates of the same kind are due from the same person and could be included in one warrant of distress, then no costs may be allowed if several warrants are used where one would be enough. In addition, a warrant of distress may provide that charges attending the distress shall be levied under the warrant to an amount authorised by statutory instrument (s 101 GRA 1967; and see Distress for Rates Order 1979, SI 1979 No 1038).

(f) Armed forces

Under s 2(2) Reserve and Auxiliary Forces (Protection of Civil Interests) Act 1951 ("RAF(PCI)A 1951") a rating authority may not proceed to levy distress against a person called up or volunteering for service in the armed forces without leave of the appropriate court. The restriction will apply in the following cases:

(i) where the person liable is for the time being performing a period of relevant service as defined in Sch I RAF(PCI)A 1951 as extended;

(ii) where the person liable has been performing a period of relevant service and while he was so doing an application for leave to exercise the remedy was made to the appropriate court;

(iii) where, on the application of the person liable, the appropriate court so directs, on being satisfied that such person is unable immediately to pay the outstanding sum by reason of circumstances directly or indirectly attributable to his or someone else's performing or having performed a period of relevant service; or

(iv) where the person liable to pay the debt has made such application to the appropriate court and the application has not been disposed of, or not having made such an application, has given to the person seeking to exercise the remedy notice of his intention to do so (s 3(1) RAF (PCI) A 1951).

The appropriate court is the court having jurisdiction to issue the warrant of distress (rr 5 and 7 RAF (PCI) R 1951).

The application for leave to proceed may be made at the hearing of a summons for non-payment of rates provided that a notice in the prescribed form has been served on the defendant not less than four clear days before the hearing.

If a warrant of distress has been issued without leave to levy the distress and leave is or subsequently becomes necessary, an application for leave may be made to the court at the hearing of a summons issued for this purpose (r 35(3) RAF (PCI) R 1951).

If a notice or summons required to be served is not served personally upon the defendant, the rating authority must, before the court decides whether to give leave to distrain, call its attention to the date and manner of service, and to any circumstances within the knowledge of the authority bearing on the question whether and when the notice or summons came to the knowledge of the defendant (r 35(4) RAF (PCI) R 1951).

Where, on an application for leave, the court is of the opinion that the person liable is unable immediately to pay by reason of circumstances directly or indirectly attributable to his or someone else's performing or having performed a period of relevant service, the court may refuse leave or give leave subject to such restrictions and conditions as it thinks proper (s 2(4) RAF (PCI) A 1951).

3. Imprisonment owing to insufficient distress

(a) Application for a warrant of commitment

Should distress prove unsuccessful, application may be made for the issue of a warrant of commitment against the person to whom the proceedings relate.

The person who holds the warrant makes the application by making a return to the court that he can find no goods or chattels (or not sufficient goods or chattels) on which to levy the sums directed to be levied. The court may then, if it thinks fit, issue a warrant of commitment (s 102 GRA 1967).

The warrant of commitment may be directed to the rating authority, to the constables of the police area in which the warrant is issued, and to such other persons, if any, as the court issuing the warrant may think fit.

General rates

The warrant may be executed anywhere in England and Wales, although before it can be issued a means inquiry must first be held (s 103 GRA 1967).

(b) Means inquiry

The presence of the person to whom the proceedings relate is required (s 103 GRA 1967). For this purpose, where a return of insufficiency of distress is made, a justice having jurisdiction in the petty sessions area in which the return is made may issue a summons to the person liable, requiring him to appear before the court (s 104(2) GRA 1967). Should the person fail to appear in answer to the summons a warrant may be issued for his arrest. Alternatively a warrant may be issued in the first instance without a summons being issued.

A warrant issued in accordance with the above provisions may be executed anywhere in the United Kingdom in the same way as a warrant issued by a magistrates' court for the arrest of an accused under s 13 MCA 1980 (s 104(2) GRA 1967). See pages 167 and 168 for the prescribed forms of summons and warrant.

(c) Hearing

The court must be composed of at least two justices or a stipendiary magistrate (s 106 GRA 1967).

A statement in writing to the effect that wages of any amount have been paid to a person during any period, purporting to be signed by or on behalf of an employer, shall be evidence of the facts stated therein (s 103(4) GRA 1967).

Even at this stage a person appearing before the court can raise the objection that he is not the rateable occupier of the premises concerned *(R v Ealing Justices, ex parte Coatsworth* (1980)).

Where no warrant of commitment is issued the court may remit the payment of any sum to which the application relates or any part of that sum (s 103(2) GRA 1967). In addition, where no warrant of commitment is issued the application may be renewed, except in relation to any sum remitted, on the ground that the circumstances of the person to whom the application relates have changed (s 103(3) GRA 1967).

(d) Period of imprisonment

The court may issue a warrant of commitment committing the person to whom the application relates to prison for a period not exceeding three months, unless the sums shown on the warrant be sooner paid (s 102(5) GRA 1967). Schedule 4 MCA 1980 does not apply, but as three months is the maximum term of imprisonment nothing should preclude its voluntary application, thus bringing it into line with all other instances of imprisonment for debt.

The court must be satisfied that the failure to pay the sum rated was due to wilful refusal or culpable neglect (s 103(1)(a) GRA 1967) otherwise it may not issue a warrant of commitment (s 103(1)(b) GRA 1967). The need to make a proper finding of culpable neglect has been reinforced in *R v Manchester City Magistrates' Court ex parte Davies* (1988). The justices found that the defendant's failure to take his accountant's advice to close his business or go bankrupt constituted culpable neglect. The High Court disagreed and observed that such a finding would be unsustainable in law. The court emphasised that it was the defendant's failure to pay which must be due to his culpable neglect. It was held that the justices, having failed to establish culpable neglect, had acted without jurisdiction and that therefore they were not entitled to the protection of s 52 Justices of the Peace Act 1979. Although the justices had acted in the execution of their office when issuing the committal warrant, the applicant had undergone a greater hardship than that assigned by law for non-payment, since a person could only be imprisoned for non-payment of rates if the precondition of blameworthiness, ie wilful refusal or culpable neglect, was present.

The warrant of commitment may be made not only for non-payment of the sum alleged to be due for rates but also for:

(i) such costs incurred in obtaining the warrant of distress as may have been included in the warrant of distress;
(ii) the charges attending the distress; and
(iii) the costs of commitment.

Where the application relates to more than one outstanding rate there is no power to impose more than one term of imprisonment *(R v Bexley Justices, ex parte Floyd Henry* (1971)). Nor may consecutive terms of imprisonment be ordered. The Magistrates' Courts Act 1980 does not apply.

See page 168 for the prescribed form of warrant of commitment.

The courts have again recently been reminded of the need to consider other methods of enforcement before issuing a warrant of commitment. In *R v Birmingham Magistrates' Court, ex parte Mansell* (1988) it was held that the justices were in error in committing a rate payer to prison for non-payment of rates when, although he had not available income to meet his debts, he had capital assets which could be sold. It was shown that the defendant could not afford to pay the weekly amounts fixed by the court, but that he had substantial capital assets to satisfy the outstanding sum. It was said that it was not open to the justices to commit the defendant to prison without having enquired whether or not the rating authority was prepared to explore the possibility of civil proceedings.

(e) Young persons

The court may not commit to prison any person who is under twenty-one years of age (s 1 CJA 1982). However, where but for this restriction the court would have power to commit to prison a person who is under twenty-one but not less than seventeen years of age for default in payment, it may instead commit him to be detained, or make an order fixing a term of detention in the event of default, for a term not exceeding the term of imprisonment (s 9 CJA 1982).

Before the court can make such an order it must:

(i) be satisfied that the failure to pay the sum rated was due to wilful refusal or culpable neglect (s 103(1)(a) GRA 1967);

(ii) be of the opinion that no other method of dealing with the defaulter is appropriate (s 1(5) CJA 1982).

Where the court does commit such person to be detained for default in payment it must state in open court the reason for its opinion that no other method of dealing with the defaulter is appropriate. Any reason given in accordance with this requirement must be specified in the warrant of commitment and entered in the court register (s 2(7) CJA 1982).

(f) Postponing the issue of the warrant of commitment

The court has power to fix a term of imprisonment and postpone the issue of the warrant of commitment on such terms as it thinks fit. Where the court exercises this power and default is made in the terms of postponement notice must be given before the warrant is issued (*R* v *Colchester Justices, ex parte Wilson* (1985)).

In *R* v *Poole Justices, ex parte Fleet* (1983) (which pre-dated the *Colchester Justices* case), it was held that where the issue of the warrant of commitment was postponed on terms, then in the event of failure to comply with the terms of postponement, the court was again under a duty to inquire, in the rate-payer's presence, whether the failure was a result of wilful refusal or culpable neglect, before the warrant was issued.

Note that the requirement is not simply one of giving notice and an opportunity of being heard. The principle established in *R v Poole* goes further than this and requires a second inquiry to determine whether the failure to pay arose from wilful refusal or culpable neglect. It should not be assumed that this necessarily conflicts with *R v Colchester Justices,* for that case was concerned primarily with the non-payment of fines, whereas the *Poole* case was concerned specifically with the non-payment of rates. It is submitted therefore that *R v Poole Justices* must be followed in addition to *R v Colchester Justices* and as a direct consequence, where the issue of a warrant for non-payment of rates is postponed, a second means inquiry is required before the warrant is issued.

(g) *Reduction of imprisonment on part-payment*

Where a period of imprisonment has been fixed and the issue of the warrant of commitment postponed, then, if the warrant falls to be issued and the total of the sums for which the warrant has been made, other than the costs of commitment, has been reduced by part payment, the period of imprisonment to be imposed is the term originally fixed reduced by such number of days as bears to the total number of days in the term less one day the same proportion as the part paid bears to that total (s 102(5) GRA 1967). Where a period of imprisonment has been imposed and part payment is made thereafter, the period of imprisonment is reduced by such number of days as bears to the total number of days shown in the warrant less one day the same proportion as the amount paid bears to so much of the sums due at the time when the period of imprisonment was imposed.

In making the required calculation under either of the above, any fraction of a day is to be left out of account.

4. Water rates

A distinction should be drawn between the following:

    (a)   water rates;
    (b)   water charges.
    (c)   drainage rates and charges.

(a) *Water rates*

A water rate is recoverable summarily as a civil debt in accordance

General rates

with the provisions of s 38(1) and (3) Water Act 1945 ("WA 1945") and not otherwise.

"Water rate" includes charges for services performed, facilities provided or rights made available by a water authority (including separate charges for separate services, facilities or rights or combined charges for a number of services, facilities or rights) (s 30 and Sch 8 para 53 Water Act 1973 ("WA 1973")).

Water rates are payable in advance by equal quarterly instalments or, if the water authority so resolves, by equal half yearly instalments (s 55 Sch 3 WA 1945). No proceedings may be commenced for the recovery of any such instalment until the expiration of two months from the first day of the half year in respect of which it has been demanded.

Before a water rate can be recovered a demand must have been made. The demand must be in writing and signed on behalf of the water authority. Service of the demand may be effected in accordance with s 56 Water Act 1945.

The procedure is by way of complaint and summons (s 58 MCA 1980). At the hearing it should be established that a demand has been served and that payment has not been effected within seven days of the demand (s 38(3) WA 1973).

The person liable to pay the rate is the occupier of the premises, except where the owner is not the occupier but is liable, by or under any enactment or by agreement with the water authority to pay the water rate for a supply of water to the premises (s 38(2) WA 1945).

The decision of the court is in the form of an order. A minute of the order must be served on the defendant before a warrant of distress can be issued (r 53(1) MCR 1981).

An attachment of earnings order cannot be made to recover a water rate, nor may imprisonment be ordered (s 1 AEA 1971). A warrant of distress may be issued (s 2 AJA 1970).

In addition to the above procedure, a water rate may be recovered as a contract debt in the county court (s 76(1) MCA 1980).

(b) Water charges

Water charges may be recovered in the same way as water rates, since they are included in the definition of "water rates" in the Water Act 1973.

Alternatively, water charges may be recovered in the same way as general rates (s 32A WA 1973). This will only apply where a local authority and water authority have entered into an agreement for the collection and recovery by the local authority on behalf of the water authority of any charges payable for services performed, facilities provided or rights made available by the water authority in the local authority's area. Where such an agreement has been entered into, charges may be recovered by the local authority in like manner as, and together with, any amount due to the local authority in respect of the general rate.

(c) Drainage rates and charges

Arrears of drainage rates may be recovered by an internal drainage board in the same manner as arrears of a general rate (s 80(1) Land Drainage Act 1976).

Arrears of any drainage charge may be recovered by a water authority in the same manner as arrears of a general rate under the General Rate Act 1967 (s 58(1) Land Drainage Act 1976).

Appendix 1

Maximum terms of imprisonment: summary

IT SHOULD BE NOTED THAT THE TERMS OF IMPRISONMENT SET OUT BELOW ARE EXPRESSED AS MAXIMA AND DO NOT REPRESENT A NORM.

Fines etc
The maximum period of imprisonment which may be imposed for non-payment of fines etc are:

Amount	
not exceeding £50	7 days
exceeding £50 but not exceeding £100	14 days
exceeding £100 but not exceeding £400	30 days
exceeding £400 but not exceeding £1,000	60 days
exceeding £1,000 but not exceeding £2,000	90 days
exceeding £2,000 but not exceeding £5,000	6 months
exceeding £5,000 but not exceeding £10,000	9 months
exceeding £10,000	12 months

Minimum period 5 days.

Maintenance
The maximum period of imprisonment which may be imposed in the event of non-payment of maintenance is as above but subject to a maximum of 42 days regardless of the arrears owed; eg maintenance arrears exceeding £100 but not exceeding £400 should not carry imprisonment in excess of 30 days. However, arrears exceeding £400 would be limited to 42 days.

Minimum period 5 days.

Legal aid
As for maintenance.

Civil debt
The maximum period of imprisonment which may be imposed in the event of non-payment of a sum enforceable as a civil debt and which is contained in Sch 4 Administration of Justice Act 1970 is

the same as for fines, but subject to a maximum term of six weeks regardless of the debt owed.

Minimum period 5 days.

Rates

The maximum period of imprisonment which may be imposed in the event of non-payment of rates is the same as for fines, but subject to a maximum term of three months regardless of the rates owed. Sch 4 MCA 1980 does not apply but nothing would preclude its voluntary application, thus bringing it into line with imprisonment for all other forms for debt.

Minimum period 5 days.

Appendix 2

Forms

Contents

Enforcement of fines, etc   *page*

1. Notice of fine   135
2. Distress warrant   136
3. Attendance centre order: non-payment of fines   136
4. Warrant of commitment on occasion of conviction   137
5. Warrant of commitment on occasion subsequent to conviction   138
6. Summons to fine defaulter   139
7. Warrant for arrest of fine defaulter   140
8. Warrant for detention in police cells, etc   141
9. Warrant for detention in police station   142
10. Transfer of fine order   143
11. Transfer of fine order to Scotland or Northern Ireland   144
12. Notice of transfer of fine order   145
13. Notice of fine supervision order   146
14. Authority for clerk of magistrates' court to enforce payment of fine in High Court or county court   146

Fixed penalties
15. Notification to fixed penalty clerk of registration of unpaid fixed penalty as a fine   147
16. Notice to defaulter of registration of unpaid fixed penalty as a fine   147
17. Statutory declaration under s 37(2) Transport Act 1982   148
18. Statutory declaration under s 37(3) Transport Act 1983   149

Enforcement of maintenance orders
19. Extract from register proving proceedings of a magistrates' court   150
20. Certificate of clerk of magistrates' court of non-payment of sums adjudged   150
21. Declaration as to non-payment of sums adjudged   151
22. Warrant of commitment for the enforcement of maintennance order or order enforceable as magistrates' court maintenance order for use in case of immediate issue   151

ENFORCEMENT IN THE MAGISTRATES' COURTS

23.	Warrant of commitment for enforcement of maintenance order enforceable as magistrates' court maintenance order for use where issue has been postponed	152
24.	Notice that warrant of commitment falls to be issued	153
25.	Application requesting that warrant should not be issued	154
26.	Application requesting that warrant should be cancelled	154
27.	Application for registration of maintenance order in a magistrates' court	155
28.	Notice that payments have become payable through the clerk of a magistrates' court	156
29.	Certificate of clerk of magistrates' court that no process for enforcement remains in force and no proceedings for variation are pending	156
30.	Notice of cancellation of registration of a High Court or county court order	157
31.	Certificate of arrears	157
32.	Notice to person liable to make payments that sums payable under a maintenance order made by a court of summary jurisdiction in England have ceased to be payable to or through any officer or person	157

Attachment of earnings

33.	Attachment of earnings order: maintenance	158
34.	Attachment of earnings order: lump sum	159
35.	Temporary variation order	160

Civil debt

36.	Complaint: civil debt	160
37.	Summons to defendant: civil debt	160
38.	Order: civil debt	161
39.	Distress warrant: civil debt	161
40.	Complaint to enforce civil debt order	162
41.	Judgment summons	163
42.	Commitment: civil debt enforceable by imprisonment	164

Rates

43.	Complaint for non-payment of rate	164
44.	Summons for non-payment of rate	165
45.	Form of distress warrant	165
46.	Form of distress warrant against several rate-payers	166
47.	Summons to rate defaulter	167
48.	Warrant for arrest of rate defaulter	168
49.	Form of warrant of commitment in default of distress	168
50.	Certificate of clerk magistrates' court that no process for enforcement remains in force	169
51.	Certificate of clerk of magistrates' court that copy of maintenance order is a true copy sent for registration.	170
52.	Notice that payments have ceased to be payable through the clerk of the magistrates' court	170
53.	Notice to person liable to make payments that sums payable under a maintenance order registered in a court of summary jurisdiction in England have become payable through collecting officer	171

Forms

1. Notice of fine (Form 46 MC(F)R 1981)

.... Magistrates' Court (Code)

Date ....

Case No ....

Convicted on .... (*date*) ....
by the [............ Magistrates' Court]
[Crown Court at ....]

Driving Licence No ....

Offence(s)	Fine	Compen-sation	Costs	Total
	£	£	£	£

You have been ordered to pay the sums shown above [by (*date*)] [by weekly/monthly instalments of £   the first instalment to be paid by (*date*)]

Payment may be made personally at the address shown below on (*days* between (*time*) and (*time*); or—

By post to the address shown below. Crossed cheques and postal orders should be made payable to the 'Justices' Clerk'. Cash should not be sent in unregistered envelopes. Any communication sent by post must be properly stamped.

Payment to The Justices' Clerk
(*Address*)

(*Telephone No*) ....)

Failure to pay in accordance with the above directions may result in a distress warrant being issued against you or a warrant for your arrest unless you have been granted further time for payment; application for further time for payment may be made in writing to the Justices' Clerk stating the grounds for the application.

NOTE: This notice should be sent with any payment or application.

2. Distress warrant (Form 48 MC(F)R 1981)

MAGISTRATES' COURT (Code)

Date:
Accused:
Address:

Offence	Fine	Compensation	Costs	Total
	£	£	£	£

was on *(date)* at [Crown Court] [Magistrates' Court] ordered to pay the sums specified above in accordance with the terms of the notice of fine served on the accused and default has been made in payment and the following sum is still outstanding:

Total amount   £
*Still outstanding:**
Direction: You [the Constables of   Police Force] [   ] are hereby required immediately to make distress of the money and goods of the accused (except the clothing and bedding of the accused and the accused's family, and to the value of fifty pounds, the tools and implements of the accused's trade); and if the amount shown above as still outstanding, together with the costs and charges of taking and keeping the distress, are not paid, then not earlier than the sixth day after the making of the distress, unless the accused consents in writing to an earlier sale, to sell the goods and pay the proceeds of the distress to the Clerk of the Magistrates' Court and if [no] [insufficient] distress can be found, to certify the same to that Magistrates' Court.

Justice of the Peace
[By order of the Court,
Clerk of the Court]

3. Attendance centre order: non-payment of fines (Form 3B Magistrates' Courts (Children and Young Persons) Rules 1988)

JUVENILE COURT *(Code)*

Date:
Defauler: Age   Years
Address:
Offence: *(Short particulars and Statute)*

Forms

Fine	The defaulter was on *(date)* adjudged to pay the total sum set out in the margin hereof
Compensation	[forthwith] [or (here see effect of order)] and has made default in payment of [the whole] [the balance set out in the margin.]
Costs	
Total	
Part payments	
Balance	

Decision: The defaulter shall attend at the attendance centre on *(date)* at *(time)* and, subsequently, at such times as shall be fixed by the officer in charge of that centre, until the accused has completed a period of attendance of   hours unless the outstanding sum is sooner paid (but see *Note 2* below).

Justice of the Peace.
[*or* By order of the Court
Clerk of the Court]

Note 1: The present address of the attendance centre specified above is:

Note 2: Under section 17(13) of the Criminal Justice Act 1982 the period of attendance may be reduced proportionately by payment of part of the outstanding sum.

4. Warrant of commitment on occasion of conviction (Form 51 MC(F)R 1981)

MAGISTRATES' COURT (*Code*)

Date:
Accused: Age: Years
Address:
Offence: *(short particulars and statute)*
Ordered to pay: £   fine
                    £   compensation
                    £   costs

[Imprisonment]
[detention] in
default of payment:

To take effect   *(state reason)*
forthwith because:

*[This court is of the opinion that no method of dealing with the accused in respect of his default other than to order his detention is appropriate because *(state reason)*].

137

ENFORCEMENT IN THE MAGISTRATES' COURTS

Direction: You, [the constables of
Police Force] [the authorised persons for
          ] [   ] are hereby required to
convey the accused to
[prison] [detention centre] [youth custody centre] and
there deliver the accused to the Governor thereof,
together with this warrant; and you, the Governor to
receive into your custody and keep the accused for that
period [to commence at the end of the term of
[imprisonment] [detention] [youth custody] (*give particulars*)] unless the amount remaining due be sooner
paid.

Justice of the Peace
[*or* By order of the Court
Clerk of the Court]

*Delete if the accused appears to have attained the age of 21 years.

5. Warrant of commitment on occasion subsequent to conviction (Form 52 MC(F)R 1981)

MAGISTRATES' COURT (*Code*)

Date:

Accused:

Addressed:

[Convicted on] [Unpaid fixed penalty registered for enforcement as a fine on]:

by the   [Magistrates' Court]
                     [Crown Court at   ]

Offence: (*short particulars and statute*)

Amount outstanding £
when [imprisonment]
[detention] imposed:

[Imprisonment]
[detention in]
default of payment   days

Imposed on:

by the: [Magistrates' Court]
                     [Crown Court at   ]

*[This court is satisfied that the default is due to the accused's wilful refusal or culpable neglect and has considered or tried all other methods of enforcing payment, namely —

(a) the making of a money payment supervision order;
(b) the making of an attachment of earnings order;
(c) the issue of a distress warrant;
(d) an application to the High Court or county court for remedies available in those courts;

Forms

(e) in the case of an offender under 21 years of age, the making of an attendance centre order,

and it appears to the court that all these methods are inappropriate or unsuccessful.] [The said offence is punishable with imprisonment and the accused appears to this court to have sufficient means to pay the amount remaining due] [the accused is already serving a term of imprisonment].

† [This court is of the opinion that no method of dealing with the accused in respect of his default other than to order his detention is appropriate because (*state reason*)].

†† [This court is satisfied that it is undesirable/impracticable to place the accused under supervision because (*state grounds)*]

Amount remaining due: £

Period to be served: days

Direction: You, [the Constables of Police Force] [the authorised persons for] [ ] are hereby required to convey the accused to [prison] [detention centre] [youth custody centre] and there deliver the accused to the Governor thereof, together with this warrant; and you, the Governor to receive into your custody and keep the accused for the said period of [to commence at the end of the term of [imprisonment] [detention] [youth custody] (*give particulars)*] unless the amount remaining due be sooner paid.

Justice of the Peace
[*or* by order of the Court
Clerk of the Court]

* Delete if a term of imprisonment has been fixed on a previous occasion.

† Delete if the accused appears to have attained the age of 21 years.

†† Delete if the accused appears to have attained the age of 21 years or has been placed under supervision.

6. Summons to fine defaulter (Form 53 MC(F)R 1981)

MAGISTRATES' COURT (*Code*)

Date:
To the accused:
Address:

Convicted on:
by the: [Magistrates' Court]
Crown Court at]

139

ENFORCEMENT IN THE MAGISTRATES' COURTS

Offence:	*(short particulars and statute)*	
Ordered to pay:	£	fine
	£	compensation
	£	costs
Total:	£	
Payments made:	£	

Amount still outstanding: £

You have failed to pay the amount shown above as still outstanding.
You are therefore hereby summoned to appear before the Magistrates' court sitting at
     on   at
unless the above amount has been paid in full beforehand, for inquiry to be made as to your means.

                                Justice of the Peace
                                  [Justices' Clerk]

Note: The purpose of the inquiry as to your means is to enable the Court to decide whether or not to commit you to prison for default in payment. If you do not pay the outstanding amount in full and fail to appear in person in answer to this summons, you will render yourself liable to arrest without further notice.

7. Warrant for arrest of fine defaulter (Form 54 MC(F)R 1981)

                                      MAGISTRATES' COURT (*Code*)

Date:
Accused:
Address:

Date penalty imposed:
by the: [Magistrates' Court]
              [Crown Court at   ]

Total amount still outstanding: £

Direction: You [the Constables of
Police Force] [the authorised persons for
               ] [   ] are hereby required to arrest the accused and bring him before the Magistrates' Court at
immediately.

* *Bail*   On arrest the accused shall be released on bail on entering into a recognizance in the sum of £   for the

Forms

accused's appearance before the last mentioned Magistrates' Court at   m. on   unless the amount outstanding be sooner paid.

Justice of the Peace

* Delete if bail is not allowed and amend as appropriate where sureties are required or conditions imposed.

8. Warrant for detention in police cells, etc (Form 57 MC(F)R 1981)

MAGISTRATES' COURT (*Code*)

Date:
Accused:
                        Age: years
Address:

Convicted on:
by the: [Magistrates' Court]
                   [Crown Court at   ]
Offence: (short particulars and statute)

Amount outstanding when imprisonment imposed: £

Imprisonment in default of payment: days

Imposed on:
by the: [Magistrates' Court]
                   [Crown Court at   ]

[(*Delete if a term of imprisonment has been fixed on a previous occasion*) [This court has considered or tried all other methods of enforcing payment and it appears to this court that they are inappropriate or unsuccessful]
[The said offence is punishable with imprisonment and the accused appears to this court to have sufficient means to pay the amount remaining due]
[The accused is already serving a term of imprisonment]]

[(*Delete if the accused appears to have attained the age of 21 years*) This court is of the opinion that no method of dealing with the accused in respect of his default other than a sentence of imprisonment is appropriate because (*state reason*)]

[(*Delete if the accused appears to have attained the age of 21 years or has been placed under supervision*) This court is satisfied that it is undesirable/impracticable to place the accused under supervision because (*state grounds*)]

Amount remaining due: £

Period to be served: days

Directions: You [the Constables of Police Force] [the authorised persons for] [ ] are hereby required to convey the accused to
 (*name of place*) and there deliver the accused to the Police Officer in charge together with this warrant; and you the Police Officer in charge to receive into your custody and keep the accused for the said period of days unless the amount remaining due be sooner paid.

Justice of the Peace
[By order of the Court,
Clerk of the Court]

9. Warrant for detention in police station (Form 58 MC(F)R 1981)

MAGISTRATES' COURT (*Code*)

Date:
Accused: *Age:* years
Address:

Offence: (short particulars and statute)

Convicted on:
by the: Magistrates' Court
Ordered to pay: £ (*Total of fine, compensation and costs*)

Amount still oustanding: £

Direction: The accused having made default in payment of the amount shown above as still outstanding:

You the constables of
Police Force are required to arrest the accused, unless the amount outstanding be sooner paid, and convey the accused to a police station and you the officer in charge of that station to detail the accused there until 8am on the day following that on which the accused is arrested between midnight and 8am until 8am on the day on which the accused is arrested provided that you the officer in charge of the police station may release the

Forms

accused at any time between 4am and 8am if you think it expedient to do so in order to enable the accused to go to work or for any other reason appearing to you to be sufficient.

Justice of the Peace
[By order of the Court,
Clerk of the Court]

10. Transfer of fine order (Form 59 MC(F)R 1981)

MAGISTRATES' COURT (*Code*)

Date:
Accused: *Age:*   years
Address:

Convicted on:
by the: [Magistrates' Court]
             [Crown Court at   ]

Total amount
ordered to pay: £   (*including fines, costs and compensation*)
Terms of payment:
Amount still
outstanding: £
[Imprisonment fixed
by the Crown Court in
default of payment:*   (Applies to Crown Court fines only)   days]

Order: This court being the court required to enforce payment of the amount shown above as still outstanding and it appears that the accused is residing at
                                                                 in the petty sessions area of
(*name area*) a transfer of fine order is hereby made under section 89 of the Magistrates' Courts Act 1980 transferring to a magistrates' court acting for that petty sessions area to the clerk of that court, all the functions under Part II of that Act in respect of the amount shown above as still outstanding.

Justice of the Peace
[Justices' Clerk]

This order should be accompanied by a statement of the offence and of the steps, if any, taken to recover the sum together with any other available information which the clerk making the order thinks is likely to assist the receiving court. Names and addresses of persons to whom costs and compensation are payable, with details of amounts, **must** *be included.*

11. Transfer of fine order to Scotland or Northern Ireland (Form 60 MC(F)R 1981)

MAGISTRATES' COURT (*Code*)

Date:
Accused: *Age:*   *years*
Address:

Convicted on:
by the: [Magistrates' Court]
             [Crown Court at   ]

Total amount
ordered to pay: £   (*including fines, costs and compensation*)
Terms of payment:
Amount still   £
outstanding:
[*Imprisonment fixed*
by the Crown Court in
default of payment: (Applies to Crown Court fines only)   days]

Order: This court being the court required to enforce payment of the amount shown above as still outstanding and it appears that the accused is residing at
                       within the jurisdiction of the court of summary jurisdiction in Scotland or Northern Ireland named below a transfer of fine order is hereby made under section 90 of the Magistrates' Courts Act 1980 transferring to the court of summary jurisdiction at
                                    (*state name and address of court*) the enforcement of payment of the amount shown above as still outstanding.

                                                Justice of the Peace
                                              [By order of the Court,
                                                  Clerk of the Court]

This order should be accompanied by a statement of the offence and of the steps, if any, taken to recover the sum together with any other available information which the clerk making the order thinks is likely to assist the receiving court. Names and addresses of persons to whom costs and compensation are payable, with details of amounts, **must** *be included.*

Forms

12. Notice of transfer of fine order (Form 61 MC(F)R 1981)

Date:
To the accused:
Address:

On   (*date*)   at   [
                    Magistrates' Court] [the Crown Court at
                    ] [a court of summary
jurisdiction in [Scotland] [Northern Ireland], namely
                    ] you were ordered to
pay the following amounts:

Fine: £
Compensation: £
Costs: £
*Amounts still
outstanding:*   £

Notice: YOU ARE HEREBY GIVEN NOTICE that in consequence of a transfer of fine order made on   (*date*) the enforcement of payment of the amount still outstanding has now become a matter for the   Magistrates' Court.

Payment of the amount outstanding should now be made to the court named below [immediately] [before   (*date*)].

If you are unable to pay you should at once make an application for [further] time to be granted by letter addressed to me setting out fully the grounds of your application.

Payment must be made personally at the address shown below   on   (*days*) between   (*time*) and (*time*) or —

By post to the address shown below. Crossed cheques and postal orders should be made payable to the "Justices' Clerk". Cash should not be sent in unregistered envelopes. Any communications sent by post must be properly stamped.

Payment to: The Justices Clerk,
                      Telephone no:

                                          Justices' Clerk

145

13. Notice of fine supervision order (Form 52 MC(F)R 1981)

MAGISTRATES' COURT (*Code*)

Date:
To the Accused:
Address:

On (*date*) at [Magistrates' Court] [the Crown Court at] you were ordered to pay the following amounts:

Fine	£
Compensation:	£
Costs	£
Amount still outstanding:	£

Notice: You are hereby given notice that you were [today] [on (*date*)] by order of this Court, placed under the supervision of (*name and address*) until you have paid the amount shown above as still outstanding or a further order be made.

[Payment is to be made by weekly/monthly instalments of £ , the first instalment to be paid immediately.]

Justices' Clerk

14. Authority for clerk of magistrates' court to enforce payment of fine in High Court or county court (Form 63 (MC(F)R 1981)

MAGISTRATES' COURT (*Code*)

Date:
Accused:
Address:
[Convicted on] [*Unpaid fixed penalty registered for enforcement as a fine on*]:
by the: [Magistrates' Court] [Crown Court at]
Offence: (*short particulars and statute*)
Ordered to pay: £ fine
£ compensation
£ costs

[This court being the court required under section 32(1) of the Powers of Criminal Courts Act 1973 to enforce payment of the sum shown above:

Forms

And] The accused having made default in payment of the amount remaining due:

Amount remaining due: £

This court having inquired into the accused's means hereby authorises the Clerk of the Court to take the undermentioned proceedings in the [High Court] [County Court] for the recovery of the amount remaining due.

Nature of proceedings:

Justice of the Peace.

15. Notification to fixed penalty clerk of registration of unpaid fixed penalty as a fine (Form 158 MC(F)R 1981)

To: The Fixed Penalty Clerk,

NOTIFICATION OF REGISTRATION

Fixed Penalty Notice No: Date Issued:
Time/Place Issued (as appropriate)
Vehicle Registration No: Driver's Licence No:
Offence:
Fixed Penalty £   Sum payable in default £

Defaulter's name:
Defaulter's address:

I hereby give notice that the above-mentioned sum payable in default of payment of a fixed penalty has been registered for enforcement as a fine against the defaulter named.

Justices' Clerk

16. Notice to defaulter of registration of unpaid fixed penalty as a fine (Form 159 MC(F)R 1981)

Date: MAGISTRATES' COURT (Code)
To   of
Notice to Owner/Hirer No: ⎱
Fixed Penalty Notice No: ⎰   Date issued:
Time/Place Issued (as appropriate)
Vehicle Registration No: *Driver's Licence No:
Offence:

You are hereby given notice that the sum of £   equal to the fixed

147

penalty payable under the notice noted above plus one half of that fixed penalty, has been registered in this Court under the authority given by sections [30(3)][32(2)] and 36(6) of the Transport Act 1982. Payment of this outstanding amount is now due and should be made either in person at the address shown below on   between   or sent by post to the address shown below. Cheques and postal orders should be crossed and made payable to the Justices' Clerk. Cash should not be sent in unregistered envelopes. Any communication sent by post must be properly stamped. The address of the court is:

   The   Magistrates' Court
   (address)

Correspondence should be addressed to the Justices' Clerk.

If you do not now pay the sum due, a distress warrant (which will permit the seizure and sale of goods to the value of the outstanding sum) may be issued against you or you may be required to appear or be arrested and brought before the court for an inquiry into your means. Application for further time for payment may be made in writing or in person to the Justices' Clerk at the above address stating the grounds of the application.

                          Justices' Clerk

Note:—This Notice should be sent/brought with any payment, enquiry or application.

17. Statutory declaration under s 37(2) Transport Act 1982 (Form 160 MC(F)R 1981)

I   (name) of
sincerely declare that:

 *A I was not the person to whom the fixed penalty notice, number   , was issued on   , in respect of vehicle, registration mark   , and for which the sum payable in default was registered as a fine on   by   Magistrates' Court.

 *B With reference to the fixed penalty notice number   issued on   , in respect of vehicle, registration mark   , and for which the sum payable in default was registered as a fine on   , by   Magistrates' Court, on   I requested a hearing in the manner specified in the fixed penalty notice.

And I make this solemn declaration conscientiously believing the same to be true, and by virtue of the provisions of the Statutory Declarations Act 1835.

 Dated   the   (date)
         (signature of person making the declaration)

 Declared before me
            (signature of Justice of the Peace)

 Name of Justice (in block letters)

*delete as applicable

Forms

Note: Any person who knowingly and wilfully makes a statutory declaration which is false in a material particular is guilty of an offence and liable on conviction to a term of imprisonment for a period of up to 2 years or to a fine or to both (section 5 of the Perjury Act 1911).

18. Statutory declaration under s 37(3) Transport Act 1982 (Form 161 MC(F)R 1981)

I   (name) of
                                           (address) do solemnly and sincerely declare that:—

*A with reference to the fixed penalty notice/notice to owner/notice to hirer number   , issued on   , in respect of vehicle, registration mark   , and for which the sum payable in default was registered as a fine on   , by   Magistrates' Court, I did not know of the fixed penalty concerned or of any fixed penalty notice/notice to owner/notice to hirer relating to that penalty until I received notice of registration.

*B I was not the owner/hirer of the vehicle, registration mark   , at the time of the alleged offence on   , of which particulars are given in notice to owner/notice to hirer number   , and for which the sum payable in default was registered as a fine on   , by   Magistrates' Court and have reasonable excuse for failing to comply with the requirements of that notice to owner/notice to hirer, namely, that

*C With reference to the notice to owner/notice to hirer number   , issued on   , in respect of vehicle, registration mark   , and for which the sum payable in default was registered as a fine on   , by   Magistrates' Court on   I requested a hearing in the manner specified by the notice to owner/notice to hirer.

And I make this solemn declaration conscientiously believing the same to be true, and by virtue of the provisions of the Statutory Declarations Act 1835.

Dated the   (date)
                                       (signature of person making the declaration)

Declared before me   (signature
                                                of Justice of the Peace)

Name of Justice (in block letters)
*delete as applicable

Note: Any person who knowingly and wilfully makes a statutory declaration which is false in a material particular is guilty of an offence and liable to conviction to a term of imprisonment for a period of up to 2 years or to a fine or to both (section 5 of the Perjury Act 1911).

19. Extract from register proving proceedings of a magistrates' court (Form 154 MC(F)R 1981)

In the [county of   Petty Sessional Division of   ].
Memorandum of a conviction [or order (or other proceeding) entered in the Register of the Magistrates' Court sitting at   , the   day of   , 19

Name of informant or of complaint	Name of defendant Age, if known	Nature of offence or matter of complaint	Date of offence or matter of complaint	Plea of consent to order	Minute of adjudication	Time allowed for payment and instalments

I certify the above extract to be a true copy.

Clerk of the said Magistrates' Court.

Dated the   day of   , 19

20. Certificate of clerk of magistrates' court of non-payment of sums adjudged (Form 146 MC(F)R 1981)

MAGISTRATES' COURT (Code)

Date
I hereby certify that the payments due to me on behalf of
from
under an order made by the
Magistrates' Court on   (*date*)
under the (State the Act under which the order was made)
have not been made to me in full and there is now in arrear the sum of £
in respect of [periodical payments] [instalments] due up to and including
           (*date*).

Justices' Clerk

Forms

21. Declaration as to non-payment of sums adjudged (Form 147 MC(F)R 1981)

I,   of,   do solemnly and sincerely declare that the payments due to me from   under an order made by the Magistrates' Court sitting at   , on the
day of   19   , under (*state the Act under which the order was made*) have not been made to me in full, and that there is now in arrear the sum of
              [in respect of periodical payments [*or* instalments] due up to and including the   day of   , 19   ].
And I make this solemn declaration, conscientiously believing the same to be true, by virtue of the provisions of the Statutory Declarations Act 1935.

(Signed)

Declared at   the   day of   , 19   ,
before me.

                                            Justice of the Peace
         for the [county] of   (*Or other description*)

22. Warrant of commitment for the enforcement of maintenance order or order enforceable as magistrates' court maintenance order for use in case of immediate issue (Form 18 MC(MOA 1958)R 1959)

In the county of   Petty Sessional Division of

To each and all of the Constables of   and to the
Governor of Her Majesty's prison at   (or the Police
Officer in charge of   ).
Whereas on a complaint made by   of   , that
             of   (hereinafter called the defendant)
had made default in payment of the sums ordered to be paid by (*insert particulars of maintenance order*) it was proved to the Magistrates' Court sitting at
           , that the defendant did owe to   of
the sum of   under the order and the sum of
              for costs thereunder.

And whereas the Court having inquired in the presence of the defendant whether the default was due to his wilful refusal or culpable neglect is not of the opinion that it was not so due.

And whereas [the Court is of opinion that it is inappropriate to make an attachment of earnings order] [there is no power to make an attachment of earnings order].

It is ordered, the defendant not being absent, that he be committed to prison (or detained in police custody) for (*state period*) unless he sooner pays the said sums due from him as aforesaid [together with the costs of enforcement] as set out below.

You the said Constables are hereby required to take the defendant and convey him to the Governor of her Majesty's prison (or the Police Officer in charge of   ) at   and you the said Governor (or Police Officer) to receive the defendant into your custody and keep him for (*state period*) from his arrest under this order or until he be sooner discharged in due course of law.

Dated the   day of   19   .

Justice of the Peace for the (*county*) first above mentioned
or by order of the court
Clerk of the Magistrates' Court sitting at

Amount found due	£
Deductions in respect of Income Tax ..	£
Net amount...	£
Enforcement costs payable	£
Total sum payable by defendant.................	£

Endorsement of payments

    Date of Receipt   £   p   *Signature*

23. Warrant of commitment for enforcement of maintenance order or order enforceable as magistrates' court maintenance order for use where issue has been postponed (Form 19 MC(MOA 1958)R 1959)

In the county of   Petty Sessional Division of

To each and all of the Constables of   and to the Governor
of Her Majesty's prison at   (or the Police Officer in charge
of   ).

Whereas on a complaint made by   of   , that
of   (hereinafter called the defendant) has made default in payment of the sums ordered to be paid by (*insert particulars of maintenance order*) it was proved to the Magistrates' Court sitting at
            , that the defendant did owe to   of
              for costs thereunder.

And whereas the Court having inquired in the presence of the defendant whether the default was due to his wilful refusal or culpable neglect is not of the opinion that it was not so due.

And whereas [the Court is of opinion that it is inappropriate to make an attachment of earnings order] [there was no power to make an attachment of earnings order].

And whereas the Court, the defendant not being absent, on the   day of   , 19   , fixed a term of imprisonment (*insert term*) and postponed issue of the warrant of commitment (*insert term of postponement* unless there has been a further postponement).

[And whereas on the application of the defendant the Court on the   day of   19   further postponed the issue of the warrant (*insert terms of further postponement*)]

[And whereas on the application of the defendant the warrant having been executed the Court cancelled the warrant of commitment but fixed a further term of imprisonment (*insert term*) and postponed issue of the further warrant of commitment (*insert terms of postponement*):]

Forms

And whereas under the said terms of postponement the said warrant fell to be issued and the Clerk of the Court gave notice to the defendant that he might make an application to the Court requesting that the warrant should not be issued.
[And whereas no such application was received by the Clerk within the prescribed period.]
[And whereas such an application was made and considered by [me] (the Court).]
[And whereas by reason of part payment the said sums remaining due from the defendant as aforesaid are reduced in amount to   ]
It is ordered that the defendant be committed to prison [or detained in police custody] for (*state period*) unless he sooner pays the said sums [remaining] due from him as aforesaid (together with the costs of enforcement as set out below.
You the said Constables are hereby required to take the defendant and convey him to the Governor of Her Majesty's prison [or the Police Officer in charge of   ] and you the said Governor [or Police Officer], to receive the defendant into your custody and keep him for (*state period*) from his arrest under this order or until he be sooner discharged in due course of law.

    Dated the   day of   , 19   .

Justice of the Peace for the (*county*) first above mentioned
or By order of the court

Clerk of the Magistrates' Court sitting at

Amount found due	£
Deductions in respect of Income Tax . . .	£
Net amount	£
Paid	£
Net amount remaining due	£
Enforcement costs payable	£
Total sum payable by defendant	£

Endorsement of payments

    Date of Receipt   £   p   *Signature*

24. Notice that warrant of commitment falls to be issued (Form 15 MC(MOA 1958)R 1959)

In the (county of   )   Petty Sessional Division of

Before the Magistrates' Court sitting at
To   of

PLEASE READ THIS NOTICE CAREFULLY

On the   day of   , 19   , this Court postponed the issue of a warrant of commitment in your case for the enforcement of (*insert particulars of maintenance order*) (*insert the terms of postponement*)].

You have failed to comply with these terms of postponement and the warrant committing you to prison for a term of   now falls to be issued unless you pay under the maintenance order [the sum] [the net sum, after making deductions in respect of income tax], of

153

If you consider that there are grounds for not issuing the warrant you may make an application to the Court on the attached form requesting that the warrant shall not be issued and stating those grounds.

If no such application is received by me on or before the   day of   19   and you fail to pay the sum referred to above the warrant will be issued.

If such an application is received by me on or before the   day of   19   it will be considered by a justice who may either refer it to the Court for further consideration or dismiss the application and issue the warrant forthwith.

Dated the   day of   , 19

    Clerk of the Magistrates' Court sitting at

25. Application requesting that warrant should not be issued (Form 16 (MC(MOA 1958)R 1959)

To the Magistrates' Court sitting at

I   of   have received the notice sent to me by the Clerk of the Court and dated the   day of   19   .

I hereby request that the warrant of commitment shall not be issued. The grounds of my request are as follows:

    Dated the   day of   19

                                                           (Signed)

    Note: This application should be delivered or sent by post to the Clerk of the Court (*insert address*).

26. Application requesting that warrant should be cancelled (Form 17 MC(MOA 1958)R 1959)

To the Magistrates' Court sitting at

I,   , hereby request that the warrant of commitment under which I am for the time being imprisoned (or otherwise detained) should be cancelled. The grounds of my request are as follows:

    Dated the   day of   19

                                                           (Signed)

Forms

27. Application for registration of maintenance order in a magistrates' court (Form 115 RSC O 105 r 8)

APPLICATION FOR REGISTRATION OF MAINTENANCE ORDER IN A MAGISTRATES' COURT

IN THE HIGH COURT OF JUSTICE
FAMILY DIVISION (DIVORCE)

DISTRICT REGISTRY
NO OF MATTER

BETWEEN   PETITIONER
AND   RESPONDENT

PLEASE COMPLETE IN BLOCK CAPITALS

The following information is given in support of my application for registration in a magistrates' court to recover the maintenance or interim maintenance due under an order dated the

1. The person who is to receive the payments (either for herself/himself or on behalf of a child) is:—

2. The person who has to make the payments is:—

3. The arrears are as follows:—

                 Arrears due   *Date arrears calculated to*   *Date of next payments*

    a) for wife/husband
    b) for the children named below:

Names of the children   *Date of Birth*   *Arrears due*   *Date arrears calculated to*   *Date of next payment*

4. (i) There are no other proceedings pending for the recovery of maintenance.   (Tick as appropriate) ☐

    or   ☐

    (ii) The following proceedings are pending for the recovery of maintenance.

If box (ii) has been ticked please give details of any writ, warrant or other process in force.

5. I would like the order registered because (*Please give your reasons*)

6. I have been asked by the Department of Health and Social Security to apply for registration because I am in receipt of Income Support (*Delete if not applicable*).

7. Please register—
       (Tick as appropriate)
   (i) the whole order   ☐
   (ii) paragraphs numbered   only   ☐
   (iii) the parts of the order listed below   ☐

155

If box (iii) has been ticked please list parts of order for registration.

8. The order is not already registered under the Maintenance Orders Act 1958.

Signed   Dated

28. Notice that payments have become payable through the clerk of a magistrates' court (Form 8 MC(MOA 1958)R 1959)

MAGISTRATES' COURT

Date:
To:
Address:

You are hereby given notice that the sums payable by you under (*insert particulars of maintenance order*) made on the   day of   19   by the [High Court] [County Court] [Court of Session] [High Court in Northern Ireland] and registered in this Court under Part I of the Maintenance Orders Act 1958, have under an order of this Court dated the   day of   19   , become payable through [me] [the Clerk of the Magistrates' Court sitting at   ].

Payments under the order (including payments in respect of any sums due at the date of the receipt by you of this notice should henceforth be sent to the Clerk of the Magistrates' Court at (*state address*).

Justices' Clerk

29. Certificate of clerk of magistrates' court that no process for enforcement remains in force and no proceedings for variations are pending (Form 3 MC(MOA 1958)R 1959)

I hereby certify that at the date of this certificate no process remains in force for the enforcement and no proceedings are pending in the Magistrates' Court for the variation of (*insert particulars of maintenance order*) made on the   day of   19   by the [High Court] [County Court] [Court of Session] [High Court in Northern Ireland] the payments whereunder are at present required to be made through me.

Dated the   day of   19

Clerk of the Magistrates' Court sitting at

Forms

30. Notice of cancellation of registration of a High Court or County Court order (Form 10 MC(MOA 1958)R 1959)

MAGISTRATES' COURT

Date:
To:
Address:

You are hereby given notice that the registration in this Court under Part I of the Maintenance Orders Act 1958, of (*insert particulars of maintenance order*) made on the   day of   19   by the [High Court] [County Court] [Court of Session] [High Court in Northern Ireland] has been cancelled.

Sums payable by you under the said order have by reason of the cancellation of the registration of the said order ceased to be payable through (*state clerk of the Magistrates' Court through whom payments have hitherto been required to be made*).

Payments under the order (including payments in respect of any sum due on the date of the receipt by you of this notice) should henceforth be paid to (*state name and address of person entitled to payments under this order*)

Justices' Clerk

31. Certificate of arrears (Form 3 MOA 1950 (SJ)R 1950)

I hereby certify that the arrears due at the date of this certificate (*insert particulars of maintenance order*) made on the   day of   19   by the Magistrates' Court sitting at (*address*), the payments whereunder are at present required to be made to [or through] me, amount to £   .

Dated the   day of   19   .

Collecting Officer of the Magistrates' Court sitting at (*address*).

32. Notice to person liable to make payments that sums payable under a maintenance order made by a court of summary jurisdiction in England have ceased to be payable to or through an officer or person (Form 2 MOA 1950 (SJ)R 1950)

In the (county of   Petty Sessional Division of   ) Magistrates' Court sitting at (*address*)

To   of

You are herby given notice that the sums payable by you under (*insert particulars of maintenance order*) made on the   day of   19   by this court have, by reason of the registration of the said order in (*state court in Scotland or Northern Ireland in which order is registered*) ceased to be payable through (or

157

ENFORCEMENT IN THE MAGISTRATES' COURTS

to) (*state officer or person through or to whom payments have hitherto been required to be made*).

Payments under the order (including payments in respect of any sums due at the date of the receipt by you of this notice) should henceforth be paid to (*state name and address of the person entitled to payments under the order*) [
unless you receive, or have meanwhile received, notice from the clerk of the said court in Northern Ireland that they are to be paid to any other person].

Dated the   day of   19

                       Clerk (and collecting officer) of the
                       Magistrates' Court at (*address*).

33. Attachment of earnings order: maintenance (Form 1 MC(AE)R 1971)

                                               PRIORITY

In the (County of   Petty Sessional Division of
)

Before the Magistrates' Court sitting at

To: of
                 of   who works at
                 as a   (Works No   ) is
required to make payments of £   a [week] under a maintenance order made on   by the (*insert court*). An application has been made for an attachment of earnings order to secure the payments and it appears that earnings are payable by you to him.

You are ordered to make out of those earnings periodical deductions in accordance with Schedule 3 to the Attachment of Earnings Act 1971. For the purpose of calculating the deductions the normal deduction rate shall be £   a [week] and the protected earnings rate shall be £   a [week].

And you are ordered to pay the sums deducted to the Clerk of [this Court] [the Magistrates' Court sitting at   (whose address is
)] as and when the deductions are made.

Dated

                               Justice of the Peace for the
                                    [county] aforesaid.
                             [or By order of the Court,
                                   Clerk of the Court.]

Note: A copy of an explanatory booklet [is enclosed] [may be obtained from the Clerk of the Court].

Indorsement on copy sent to debtor

This is a copy of an attachment of earnings order directed to your employer. If you leave this employment or become employed or re-employed, you must notify the Court in writing within seven days, giving particulars of your earnings and anticipated earnings from any new employment.

Failure to do so may render you liable to a fine.

Forms

34. Attachment of earnings order: lump sum (Form 2 MC(AE)R 1971)

PRIORITY

In the (County of   )   Petty Sessional Division of

Before the Magistrates' Court sitting at

To: of
              of   who works at
             as a   (Works No   ) is
required to pay a sum to which section 1(3)(b) or (c) of the Attachment of Earnings Act 1971 applies and it appears that earnings are payable by you to him.

You are ordered to make out of those earnings periodical deductions in accordance with Schedule 3 to the Attachment of Earnings Act 1971 until the amount of that sum remaining unpaid, namely £   , [on the date of this variation of an earlier order], has been deducted. For the purposes of calculating the deductions the normal deduction rate shall be £   a [week], and the protected earnings rate shall be £   a [week].

And you are ordered to pay the sums deducted to the Clerk of this Court as and when the deductions are made.

Dated

> Justice of the Peace for the
> [county] aforesaid.
> [or By order of the Court,
> Clerk of the Court.]

Note: A copy of an explanatory booklet [is enclosed] [may be obtained from the Clerk of the Court].

Indorsement on copy sent to debtor

This is a copy of an attachment of earnings order directed to your employer. If you leave this employment or become employed or re-employed, you must notify the Court in writing within seven days, giving particulars of your earnings and anticipated earnings from any new employment.

Failure to do so may render you liable to a fine.

35. Temporary variation order (Form 3 MC(AE)R 1971)

In the (County of   )   Petty Sessional Division of

To   of

An attachment of earnings order made by the Magistrates' Court sitting at   in respect of   of
                      (hereinafter called the defendant) who works at
             as a   (Works No.   )
has been served on you and the defendant has applied for a temporary variation in the order.

You are ordered to make deductions under that order as if it specified as in the protected earnings rate an increased rate of £   a [week].

159

This variation shall remain in force for a period of [four] weeks.

Dated

                                  Justice of the Peace for the [county] aforesaid.
                      [or   Justices' Clerk.]

Note: On the expiry of this temporary variation order, deductions should be made in accordance with the attachment of earnings order.

36. Complaint: civil debt (Form 104 MC(F)R 1981)

                                                            MAGISTRATES' COURT (Code)

Date:

Defendant:

Address:

Matter of
complaint: *(State grounds of complaint)*

The complaint of:

Address: Telephone no:

who [upon oath] states that the defendant was responsible for the matter of complaint of which particulars are given above and claims from the defendant the following sum which is recoverable summarily as a civil debt:

Debt: £

Taken [and sworn] before me

                                                                   Justice of the Peace
                                                                      [Justices' Clerk]

37. Summons to defendant: civil debt (Form 105 MC(F)R 1981)

                                                            MAGISTRATES' COURT (Code)

Date:

To the defendant:

of:

YOU ARE HEREBY SUMMONED to appear, unless the sum specified below be sooner paid, before the   Magistrates' Court sitting at

on   *(date)* at   m to answer to the following complaint:

Matter of
complaint: *(State grounds of complaint)*

Forms

	and that you have failed to pay the following sums which are recoverable summarily as a civil debt:
Debt:	£
Costs:	£
Complainant:	
Address:	
Date of complaint:	

Justice of the Peace
[Justices' Clerk]

38. Order: civil debt (Form 106 MC(F)R 1981)

MAGISTRATES' COURT (Code)

Date:
Defendant:
Address:
Complainant:
Address:

On the complaint of:

Matter of complaint:

(*State grounds of complaint*)

it is adjudged that the complaint is true and it is ordered:

Order:

that the defendant pay to the complainant the sum of [being an amount recoverable summarily as a civil debt and] for costs.
Payment is to be made [by weekly/monthly instalments of the first instalment to be paid] [immediately] [not later than (*date*)].

[And it is ordered that in default of payment the sum due be levied by distress and sale of the goods of the defendant.]

Justice of the Peace
[By order of the Court,
Clerk of the Court]

39. Distress warrant: civil debt (Form 109 MC(F)R 1981)

MAGISTRATES' COURT (Code)

Date:
Debtor:
Address:

ENFORCEMENT IN THE MAGISTRATES' COURTS

Amount ordered to be paid: £   being money recoverable summarily as a civil debt.

Costs: £

The debtor was on
(date) at [Magistrates' Court] [the Crown Court at
             ] ordered to pay the sums specified above [by weekly/monthly instalments of £   , the first instalment to be paid] [immediately]
[by   ]
The debtor has been served with a copy of a minute of the order and default has been made in payment:

Total amount still outstanding: £

Direction: You [the constables of
Police Force] [   ] are hereby required immediately to make distress of the money and goods of the accused (except the clothing and bedding of the accused and the accused's family, and to the value of fifty pounds, the tools and implements of the accused's trade); and if the amount shown above as still outstanding, together with the costs and charges of taking and keeping the distress, are not paid, then not earlier than the sixth day after the making of the distress, unless the accused consents in writing to an earlier sale, to sell the goods and pay the proceeds of the distress to the Clerk of the
                              Magistrates' Court and if [no] [insufficient] distress can be found to certify the same to that Magistrates' Court.

Justice of the Peace
[By order of the Court,]
Clerk of the Court]

40. Complaint to enforce civil debt order (Form 107 MC(F)R 1981)

MAGISTRATES' COURT (Code)

Date:
Debtor:
Address:

The complaint of:
Address:
                                                      Telephone no:
who [upon oath] states that on
(date)
the debtor was ordered by the [
             Magistrates' Court] [Crown Court at

Forms

	the following sum[s]:	] to pay the complainant
Sum[s] ordered to be paid:	£	
Costs:	£	to be paid
	and the debtor has made default in payment.	
Amount paid:	£	
Total amount outstanding:	£	
Amount of default:	£	
	Taken [and sworn] before me	

Justice of the Peace
[Justices' Clerk]

41. Judgment summons (Form 108 MC(F)R 1981)

MAGISTRATES' COURT (Code)

Date:

To:

of:

Matter of complaint: that on *(date)* at Magistrates' Court] [the Crown Court at] you were ordered to pay to the complainant the sum shown below and that you have made default in payment of that sum.

Complainant:

of:

Amount ordered to be paid:	£
Costs:	£
Amount paid:	£
Amount still outstanding:	£
Amount of default:	£

YOU ARE HEREBY SUMMONED to appear on *(date)* at m before the Magistrates' Court sitting at to answer to the above complaint and for inquiry to be made as to the means you have had since the order for payment was made to pay the sum or any instalment of it, and to show cause why you should not be committed to prison in accordance with section 96 of the Magistrates' Courts Act 1980, in default of payment.

Justice of the Peace
[Justices' Clerk]

163

42. Commitment: Civil debt enforceable by imprisonment (Form 110 MC(F)R 1981)

MAGISTRATES' COURT (Code)

Date:
Debtor:
Address:

Was on *(date)* by the [Crown [Magistrates'] Court at ordered to pay the sum[s] shown below:
£
£ costs
of which there is still outstanding the sum of

Amount still outstanding

£
The court is satisfied that the debtor [has] [has had since the date of the above order] the means to pay the sum [now] due and [refuses or neglects] [has refused or neglected] to pay the sum.
[It appears that [no] [insufficient] distress could be found upon which to levy the sum due.]

Decision:

that the debtor be [committed to prison] [detained in police custody] for:
unless the amount outstanding together with the costs are sooner paid.

Direction:

You [the constables of Police Force] [ ] are hereby required to take the debtor and convey him to Prison] [
] and there deliver the debtor to the [Governor] [Police officer in charge] thereof and you the [Governor] [Police officer in charge] to receive the debtor into your custody and keep the debtor for *(state period)* from the debtor's arrest under this order or until the debtor be sooner discharged in due course of law.

Justice of the Peace
[By order of the Court,
Clerk of the Court]

43. Complaint for non-payment of rate (Form A GRA 1967)

In the (County of   Petty Sessional Division of
)
The complaint of *(insert name of rating authority or persons acting for them)* who state that   , being a person duly rted and assessed by [them] in a rate made on   in the sum of £   has not paid the said sum or any part of it.

Forms

Taken before me this   day of   , 19   .
                                              Justice of the Peace for the
                                              [county] first above mentioned.

Notes:
1. Complaints for non-payment of rates by two or more persons may be combined in a single document.
2. This and the following Forms may be adapted to meet a case where a person is in default as to part only of the sum to which he was rated.

44. Summons for non-payment of rate (Form B GRA 1987)

In the (County of   Petty Sessional Division of
)
To   of
Complaint has this day been made to me, the undersigned Justice of the Peace by
           of   in the said [county] of
                       that you, being a person duly rated and assessed in a rate made on   in the sum of £   have not paid that sum or any part of it:

You are therefore hereby summoned to appear on   day the   day of   19   at the hour of   in the   noon, before the Magistrates' Court sitting at   to show cause why you have not paid the said sum.

If you do not appear you will be proceeded against as if you had appeared and be dealt with according to law.

Dated the   day of   19
                                              Justice of the Peace for the
                                              [county] first above mentioned

45. Form of distress warrant (Form C(1) GRA 1987)

In the (County of   , Petty Sessional Division of
)
To (*insert name of rating authority*) and to each and all of the Constables of

On   19   complaint was made by
that   being a person duly rated and assessed in a rate made on   19   in the sum of £   had not paid that sum or any part thereof:

And on   19   at
the complainants [and the said   have appeared before the Magistrates' Court sitting at   [but the said   has not so appeared and it has been satisfactorily proved that he was duly served with a summons so to appear]:

165

And it being now duly proved to the Court on oath [in the presence of the said   ] that the said   was assessed at the sum of £   in a rate dated   and duly made and published and that the said sum has been duly demanded from the said   but that he has not paid it:

And the said   not showing any sufficient cause for not paying the said sum:

You are hereby commanded forthwith to make distress of the goods and chattels of the said   and if within [five] days after the making of the distress the sums set out below (together with the lawful charges for taking and keeping the said distress) are not paid, to sell the said goods and chattels distrained by you and out of the proceeds of the sale to retain the said sums set out below, together with the lawful charges for taking, keeping and selling the said distress, and paying over any balance on demand to the said   ; and if no such distress can be found you are to certify that fact to the Court.

Dated the   day of   19

Justice of the Peace for the
[county] first above mentioned.

Particulars

1. Sum due for rate ....£
2. For costs of obtaining warrant of distress ....£
    Total ....£

46. Form of distress warrant against several rate-payers (Form C(2) GRA 1967)

In the (County of   Petty Sessional Division of   ).

To (*insert name of rating authority*) and to each and all of the Constables of
On   19   complaint was made by   that the persons whose names are given in the particulars at the foot of this warrant, being persons duly rated and assessed in the respective amounts set out in those particulars by rates made on the dates there set out had not paid those sums or any part thereof:

And   on   19   at   the complainants and (*names of parties who have appeared*) have appeared before the Magistrates' Court sitting at   [but the [other] persons whose names are given in the particulars at the foot of this warrant have not so appeared and it has been satisfactorily proved to the Court that the said persons not so appearing have been duly served with a summons in that behalf]:

And it being now duly proved to the Court on oath in the presence of the parties so appearing that the said persons named in the said particulars were assessed at the respective amounts there set out by the rates made as there specified and duly published and that those sums have been duly demanded from the said persons respectively but that they have not paid them or any part thereof:

And the said persons not showing any sufficient cause for not paying the said sums:

You are hereby commanded forthwith to make distress of the goods and chattels of the said persons and if within [five] days after the making of the distress the respective sums set out in the said particulars (including in each case the sums for costs there specified and the lawful charges for taking and keeping the said

Forms

distress) are not paid, to sell the goods and chattels of the parties in default distrained by you and out of the proceeds of sale to retain the respective sums so specified, together with the lawful charges for taking, keeping and selling the distress, and in each case paying over any balance on demand to the person whose goods and chattels have been so sold; and if no such distress can be found in the case of any of the said persons you are to certify that fact to the Court.

Dated the   day of   19

                                              Justice of the Peace for the
                                              [county] first above mentioned.

		Particulars			
Name of Ratepayer	*Residence*	*Rate dated*	*Arrears under rate dated*	*Costs*	*Total*

47. Summons to rate defaulter (Form 102 MC(F)R 1981)

MAGISTRATES' COURT (*Code*)

Date:
To the Defendant:
Address:

You are hereby summoned to appear, unless the sum specified below be sooner paid, before the Magistrates' Court at   on (*date*) at (*time*)   m for inquiry as to your conduct and means in relation to the non-payment of rates and costs as follows:

Rate arrears and costs   £

Rate period:

Payable to: Council that Council having applied for a warrant for your committal to prison for default in payment of that sum.

Justice of the Peace
[Justices' Clerk]

Note: If the arrears and costs outstanding are paid to before the date of hearing you need not attend the court.
If the arrears and costs are not paid and you fail to attend the court a warrant may be issued for your arrest.

167

48. Warrant for arrest of rate defaulter (Form 103 MC(F)R 1981)

MAGISTRATES' COURT (Code)

Date:
Defendant:
Address:
        is required to appear before the Magistrates' Court for inquiry as to the defendant's conduct and means in relation to the non-payment of rates and costs as follows:

Rates arrears and costs:
    £
    £   costs

Rate period:
Payable to:
        Council and that Council has applied for a warrant for the committal of the defendant to prison for default in payment of that sum.

Direction: You the constables of
Police Force are hereby required to arrest the defendant and bring him before the
Magistrates' Court immediately unless the arrears and costs are sooner paid.

Bail: (*Delete if bail is not granted*) On arrest the defendant shall be released on bail on entering into a recognizance in the sum of £   for the defendant's appearance before the above-mentioned Magistrates' Court on   (*date*) unless the arrears and costs are sooner paid.

                                              Justice of the Peace

49. Form of Warrant of commitment in default of distress (Form D GRA 1967)

In the (County of   Petty Sessional Division of
).
To each and all of the Constables of   and to the Governor of Her Majesty's prisons at
On   19   , complaint was made by
that   , being a person duly rated and assessed in a rate made on 19   , in the sum of £   , had not paid that sum or any part thereof:
and on   19   at
the complainants [and the said   ] appeared before the Magistrates' Court sitting at   [but the said   did not appear before the Court and it was satisfactorily proved that he was duly served with a summons so to appear]:
And it was duly proved to the Court on oath [in the presence of the said   ] that the said   was assessed at the sum of £   by a rate dated

Forms

and duly made and published, and that the said sum had been duly demanded from the said   , but that he had not paid it.

And the said   not showing any sufficient cause for not paying the said sum, the Court issued a warrant to   commanding them to levy the said sum together with the sum for the costs of obtaining that warrant set out below, by distress and sale of the goods and chattels of the said

And it appearing that no sufficient distress on which to levy the said sums could be found:

And inquiry having been made by the competent Court in the presence of the said   as to whether his failure to pay the said sums was due either to his wilful refusal or his culpable neglect, and that Court not being of opinion that the failure of the said   was not so due:

It is ordered that the said   be committed to prison for unless the said sums together with the further costs and charges set out below are sooner paid.*

You, the said Constables, are hereby required to take the said   and convey him to the Governor of Her Majesty's prison at   and you, the said Governor, to receive the said   into custody and imprison him for (*state period*) or until he be sooner discharged in due course of law.

Dated the   day of   19 .

Justice of the Peace for the
[county] first above mentioned.

Particulars

1. Sum due for rate .... £
2. For costs of obtaining warrant of distress .... £
3. Sum payable for the fees, charges and expenses attending
   the distress .... £
4. Costs of commitment .... £

Total .... £

*Note: The period of detention will be reduced as provided by section 102(5) of the General Rate Act 1967 if part payment is made of the sum due.

50. Certificate of clerk of magistrates' court that no process for enforcement remains in force (Form 2) *(s 2(4)(c) MOA 1958)*

I hereby certify that at the date of this certificate no process remains in force for the enforcement of (*insert particulars of maintenance order*) made on   day of   19   by the Magistrates' Court sitting at   , the payments whereunder are at present required to be made to me.

Dated the   day of   19

Clerk of the Magistrates' Court sitting at

169

51. Certificate of clerk of magistrates' court that copy of maintenance order is a true copy sent for registration (Form 7)
(s 2(4)(c) MOA 1958)

I hereby certify that this is a true copy of (*insert particulars of maintenance order*) and that it is sent to   in accordance with the provisions of paragraph (c) of subsection (4) of section two of the Maintenance Orders Act 1958, and of Rule 3 to the Magistrates' Courts (Maintenance Orders Act 1958) Rules 1959.

Dated the   day of   19

Clerk of the Magistrates' Court sitting at

52. Notice that payments have ceased to be payable through the clerk of the magistrates' court (Form 9)
(s 2(5) MOA 1958; s 19(4) MOA 1950)

MAGISTRATES' COURT (CODE)

Date:

To:

Address:

You are hereby given notice that the sums payable by you under (*insert particulars of maintenance order*) made on the   day of   19   by [this Court] (*state court in Scotland or Northern Ireland which made the order*) and registered in this Court (under Part II of the Maintenance Orders Act 1950) have by reason of the registration of the said order in the High Court ceased to be payable to (*state clerk of magistrates' court to whom payments have hitherto been required to be made*).

Payments under the order (including payments in respect of any sums due at the date of the receipt by you of this notice) should henceforth be paid to (*state name and address of the persons entitled to payments under this order*).

Justices' Clerk

Forms

53. Notice to person liable to make payments that sums payable under a maintenance order registered in a court of summary jurisdiction in England have become payable through collecting officer (Form 1 MOA 1950 (SJ)R 1950) *(s 19(4) MOA 1958)*

MAGISTRATES' COURT (CODE)

In the (county of Petty Sessional Division of)
Court of Summary Jurisdiction sitting at
To of

You are hereby given notice that the sums payable by you under (*insert particulars of maintenance order*) made on the day of 19 by (*state court in Scotland or Northern Ireland which made the order*) and registered in this Court under Part II of the Maintenance Orders Act 1950, have, under an order of this Court dated the day of 19 become payable through (or to) the Collecting Officer of this Court (or the Court of Summary Jurisdiction sitting at).

Payments under the order (including payments in respect of any sums due at the date of the receipt by you of this notice) should henceforth be sent to me (or to the said Collecting Officer) at (*state address*).

Dated the day of 19

Justices' Clerk

Index

Administration order under Insolvency Act 1986 24
Affiliation order or order enforceable as such, jurisdiction in
    respect of 55–56
    See also *Maintenance order(s)*
Aliment 87
Alimony – see *Maintenance order(s)*
Appeals 52, 63
Armed forces, member of:
    distress warrant against 66, 123–124
    financial penalty, enforcement of against 23–24
    legal aid contribution order, enforcement of against 111
    maintenance order, enforcement of against 64–67
Arrears, notification of 54
Attachment of earnings order(s) 91–107
    application for 92–93
    circumstances in which appropriate 69, 70, 94–95
    consolidation of 104–105
    discharge of 103
    duty of debtor under 97–98
    earnings, meaning of for purposes of 91–92, 103,–104
    employer's liability under 96–97, 106
    failure to comply with 98
    lapse/cessation 102–103, 105–106
    normal deduction rate under 95, 96, 97, 100
    priority of 106–107
    procedure for 92–94
    protected earnings rate under 95, 96, 97
    service of 107
    variation and discharge of 99–102
Attendance centre order 19–21

Bankruptcy, effect of on enforcement of maintenance order 51

Charging order 21–22
Child, maintenance of – see *Maintenance order(s)*
Civil debt 113–119
    sum(s) enforceable as 115–116
    sum(s) recoverable as 113–115
Commitment, warrant of 28–32, 37
    cancellation of 74–76
    execution of 36, 90
    issue of 36, 72–73, 74

Index

non-payment of confiscation order, for	40, 41
postponement of	28–29, 71–73, 74, 76, 118, 127–128
preconditions for	30–32
Company, fine on	24
Compensation order(s)	1–25
attachment of earnings order, enforcement of, by	91–107
See also *Attachment of earnings order(s)*	
distress warrant, enforcement of, by	10–15
See also *Distress, warrant of*	
High Court/county court, enforcement of, in	21–22
imprisonment/detention for non-payment of	26–38
See also *Imprisonment/detention*	
money payments supervision order, enforcement of, by	8–10
notice before enforcement of	2–3
payment of by instalments	3–4
priority of over confiscation order	42
review of	17–18
time for payment of	3–4
transfer of	4–8
Complaint to enforce maintenance arrears	55
Confiscation order(s)	39–43
Conviction, sum adjudged to be paid on	1–25
See also *Costs Order(s); Compensation order(s); Fine(s); Forfeited recognizance(s)*	
Coroner, fine imposed by	24
Costs order(s)	1–25
attachment of earnings order, enforcement of, by	91–107
See also *Attachment of earnings order(s)*	
distress warrant, enforcement of, by	10–15
See also *Distress, warrant of*	
High Court/county court, enforcement in	21–22
imprisonment/detention for non-payment of	26–38
See also *Imprisonment/detention*	
instalments, payment of, by	3–4
money payments supervision order, enforcement of, by	8–10
notice before enforcement of	2–3
time for payment of	3–4
transfer of	4–8
County court:	
enforcement in	21–22
legal aid contribution, recovery of, in	111
order, registration of in magistrates' court	78–80
Court register, record of enforcement proceedings, in	22–23
Crown Court fine	15
Death, effect of on enforcement of maintenance order	51
Debt, attachment of	21–22
See also *Civil debt*	
Distress, warrant of	10–15
armed forces, member of, against	66, 123–124

execution of 11–13
imprisonment where distress levied under is insufficient 124–128
issue of 11–13
master of boat etc, against 13–14
non-payment of civil debt, for 116
non-payment of rates, for 120–124
notice of 14–15
Domestic proceedings, enforcement of maintenance order(s)
   treated as 58–59
Drainage rates 130
Drug trafficking 39–41

Earnings, attachment of – see *Attachment of earnings order(s)*
Enforcement officer(s) 24–25

Fine(s) 1–25
   amount of 1
   attachment of earnings, enforcement of, by 91–107
      See also *Attachment of earnings order(s)*
   company, on 24
   coroner, imposed by 24
   Crown Court, imposed by 15
   distress warrant, enforcement of, by 10–15
      See also *Distress, warrant of*
   High Court/county court, enforcement of, in 21–22
   imprisonment/detention for non-payment of 26–38
      See also *Imprisonment/detention*
   money payments supervision order, enforcement of, by 8–10
   notice before enforcement of 2–3
   payment of by instalments 3–4
   registration of fixed penalty as 44–48
   remission of 16
   time for payment of 3–4
   transfer of 4–8
Fixed penalties 44–48
Forfeited recognizance(s) 1–25
   attachment of earnings order, enforcement of, by 91–107
      See also *Attachment of earnings order(s)*
   distress warrant, enforcement of, by 10–15
      See also *Distress, warrant of*
   High Court/county court, enforcement of, in 21–22
   imprisonment/detention for non-payment of 26–38
      See also *Imprisonment/detention*
   money payments supervision order, enforcement of, by 8–10
   notice before enforcement of 2–3
   payment of by instalments 3–4
   remission of 16–17
   time for payment of 3–4
   transfer of 4–8
Forms (listed at page 133) .... 135 et seq

Index

Garnishee proceedings 21–22
General rates – see *Rates*

Her Majesty's Forces – see *Armed forces, member of*
High Court:
    enforcement in 21–22
    legal aid contribution, recovery of, in 111
    magistrates' court order, registration of, in 80–82
    order, registration of in magistrates' court 78–80

Imprisonment/detention 26–38
    civil debt, for non-payment of 116–119
    confiscation order, for non-payment of 39–41
    consecutive periods of 27–28, 38, 42, 80
    effect of on liability to pay 53–58, 70–71
    insufficient distress, owing to 124–128
    maintenance order, for non-payment of 68–76
    ordered at time of conviction 29–30
    payment following imposition of 34–118
    preconditions for 30–32
    short period, for 34–35
    term of 26–27, 32–34, 70, 118, 125–126, 131
    young person, of 36–38, 69–70, 127
Income tax 54–55
Instalments, variation of payments by 3–4

Juvenile, enforcement against parent/guardian of 18–19

Legal aid contribution order(s) 108–112
    attachment of earnings order as means of enforcement of 91–107
        See also *Attachment of earnings order(s)*
    recovery from person other than the legally aided person 111–112
Lump sum order 81, 82

Magistrates' court:
    order of, registration of in High Court 80–82
    registration of county court order in 78–80
    registration of High Court order in 78–80
Maintenance order(s) 49–90
    appeals in connection with enforcement of 63
    armed forces, member of, enforcement against 64–67
    attachment of earnings as means of enforcement of 91–107
        See also *Attachment of earnings order(s)*
    costs of enforcement of 62
    domestic proceedings, treated as 58–59
    feasibility of enforcement of 51–53
    imprisonment for non-payment of 68–76
        See also *Imprisonment/detention*
    marriage, dissolution of, effect on 51
    meaning of 49–51, 77

ENFORCEMENT IN THE MAGISTRATES' COURTS

    payment of arrears under, effect of 58, 76
    procedure for enforcement of 53–62
    registration of for enforcement 53, 77–90
        See also *Registration, maintenance order, of*
    remission of arrears under 60–62, 73–74, 75
    time for enforcement of 58
    transfer of proceedings for enforcement of 56–57
Means inquiry 3–4, 14, 16, 21, 30–32, 59–60
Money payments supervision order 8–10

Northern Ireland:
    maintenance order made in, registration of in England
        and Wales 87–90
    registration of order in 83–87
Notice:
    arrears, of 54
    means inquiry, of 4
    requirement of before enforcement 2–3

Parent/guardian, enforcement against 18–19
Part payment, effect of 21, 33–34, 128
Periodical payments – see *Maintenance order(s)*

Rates, enforcement of 120–130
Receiver:
    appointed by way of equitable estoppel 22
    appointed under Insolvency Act 1986 .... 40–41, 43
Recognizance – see *Forfeited recognizance(s)*
Records of enforcement proceedings 22–23
Registration:
    fixed penalty as fine, of 44–48
    maintenance order, of, for enforcement 77–90
        cancellation of 79–80, 86–87, 89–90
        Northern Ireland, in 83–87
        Scotland, in 83–87
Remission:
    fine, of 16
    maintenance arrears, of 60–62, 73–74, 75
    recognizance, of 16–17

Scotland:
    maintenance order made in, registration of in England and
        Wales 87–90
    registration of English order in 83–87
Search of defaulter 18, 62
Services – See *Armed forces, member of*
Supervision order – see *Money payments supervision order*

Index

Transfer:
    enforcement proceedings, of 56–57, 111
    fine, of 4–8

Warrant – see *Commitment, warrant of; Distress, warrant of*
Water:
    charges 129–130
    rates 128–129
Winding-up order 24

Young person(s) 10, 36–38, 69–70, 127
    See also *Juvenile*